Birth, Death, and Resurrection

BIRTH, DEATH, AND RESURRECTION

Teaching Spiritual Growth Through the Church Year

Judy Gattis Smith

Abingdon Press

Nashville

BIRTH, DEATH, AND RESURRECTION

Teaching Spiritual Growth Through the Church Year

Library of Congress Cataloging-in-Publication Data

Smith, Judy Gattis, 1933-
    Birth, Death, and Ressurection: Teaching Spiritual Growth Through the Church Year/Judy Gattis Smith.
    p. cm.
ISBN 0-687-03550-3 (alk. paper)
    1. Church year. 2. Spiritual life—Methodist authors. I. Title.
BV30.S56 1989
263' .9—dc20   89-31464
                                                                      CIP

For my sister, Gloria

FOREWORD

So much goes into the writing of even the simplest book. There are so many people to thank in the creation of this one. First, a multitude of writers I have never met have influenced my thinking. John Westerhoff and Joseph Russell were particularly helpful in thinking about the Church Year. My husband, David, and I share so many ideas and experiences I am not sure which are mine and which are his. I know the Maundy Thursday service here is his creation, and we have used it for many years. A trip to Bombay, India, an exchange pulpit in England, the World Methodist Conference in Kenya—all gave me straw for my bricks. The children and youth in our local United Methodist church must be thanked for their enthusiastic participation in many of these experiences. Christian educators and Sunday school teachers of various denominations whom I have met in workshops around the country have given generously of their ideas and insights. I didn't know until I began writing how crucial is the role of an editor. Gregory Michael is to be thanked for his help on this book. And heartfelt thanks go to you, the readers, whose support has encouraged me to continue writing.

CONTENTS

BIRTH, DEATH, AND RESURRECTION

INTRODUCTION

There is a rumbling down deep that something different is taking place in churches of the Reformed and Free traditions. More and more ministers are preaching from a common lectionary (with Episcopalians and Roman Catholics). Colors are appearing on pulpits and lecterns—red and green, purple and white. New terms are becoming familiar in the church vocabulary—"Epiphany" and "Lent," "All Saints" and "Advent." "The Church Year" is no longer an unfamiliar expression. Those of us who grew up celebrating only Christmas and Easter are coming to a new appreciation of the rich tapestry of an entire year focused on events around the life of Christ that we are discovering through worship.

But Christian education has not kept up with this accelerated pace of accepting the Church Year. Christian educators from non-liturgical traditions often wonder how our denominational programs, our courses of study, our individual church emphasis, and even our fund-raising programs can fall under the Church Year umbrella. We don't want to just add another program to our already overcrowded schedules.

This book is for Christian educators and teachers and is an affirmation that the Church Year does indeed have a place in Christian education of the Reformed and Free traditions.

But our celebration of the Church Year in our church schools and educational programs will be different from the celebration in liturgical churches.

For one thing, we are pragmatic Protestants. We want our program of Christian education to be useful and meaningful in modern church life. We are proud of our strong heritage of Christian education. Planted deep within us are the seeds of our Puritan background which say, "Beware of anything that takes you too far from the preached and studied Word of God." Deeper than logic is a feeling that anything too ritualistic, formal, or sacerdotal will hinder us from experiencing God, and will come between us and God. We seek a transparency for reality in God, not a form that draws attention to itself.

But just as we are learning in modern medicine that extreme surgery is not always the best solution, we are coming to see that in our program of Christian education the

Church Year has much to offer non-liturgical churches and need not be discarded in its entirety.

The Church Year will become for us a means, never an end. It is a peg on which to hang our spiritual experiences and our religious understandings.

Many of us deeply love the Sunday school and have given our lives to maintaining it. We will preserve our structure, but will look carefully and thoughtfully at how an understanding of the Church Year can nurture and deepen aspects of our spiritual life and study.

We begin with an understanding of just what is the Church Year. We search for the whole picture—for the grasp of the entire cycle of the Church Year, not just sticking programs, such as Advent Workshops and Ash Wednesday Services, into our regular schedule like acupuncture needles.

Our emphasis is on the human experience, condition, or feeling that a particular season addresses. We shy away from formality that will separate us from God, but rush forward to embrace a celebration that addresses a genuine hurt or dream or concern. We study until we understand the rhythm of the entire Church Year and the variety and freshness this rhythm can bring to our program.

Next we consider the faith stories. Christian educators have long known the value of a story. What are the stories the Church Year tells? Which stories in which season? We have an ideal setting in the church school for bringing these stories alive by singing and dancing and dramatizing them.

Third, we look carefully at the programs that now make up our Christian education ventures. Which ones shall we keep? Which discard? Which work well with the Church Year? A careful assessment of these questions will make your church school unique. We value our traditions but remain open to innovation. We seek to glean the riches of the Church Year but keep our own unique programs that speak to us with power.

Yes, we can have our cake and eat it, too. We hope this book will give you some suggestions as to how.

UNDERSTANDING THE CHURCH YEAR

What is the Church Year?

The vast concept of Time is so beyond our understanding that we search for a shape to contain it, a ruler to measure it, a rhythm in which to live it. Throughout history humans have searched for a symbol that represents the concept of Time. From the Western tradition comes the symbol of Time as a journey, a pilgrimage. From the Eastern tradition comes the symbol of Time as an unfolding flower, an endlessly turning wheel. Whatever symbol speaks to us, we show by how we use this precious gift of Time what we value and consider important. The rhythm of days is deeply implanted in us.

Murray in the film *A Thousand Clowns* says, "You gotta know what day it is. If you don't know what day it is, the days just go right by and you lose them."

In the church, one method of "knowing what day it is" is the Church Year. The Church Year (or church calendar) arranges for the proclamation and observance of a balanced biblical message in a yearly sequence. The Church Year is a cycle of seasons centering on Christ, his meaning, and his message.

In non-liturgical churches, we have often associated the Church Year with special ceremonies, vestments, colors, and so on; but at its core, the Church Year is simply the cycle, the life of Christ through the calendar. All the other things are accoutrements and grace notes. We use them only if they speak to us with power.

Following the yearly cycle takes us to mountaintops and valleys of faith experiences, speaking to every human condition. As we get a feel for the entire cycle of the Church Year, we have a foundation that gives us balance and direction. What we are trying to do is not become a liturgical church, but take from the liturgical tradition what can bring us closer to God.

Like a circle going around and around, we can jump into the Church Year at any point. The Church Year begins for many at Easter, our greatest celebration. For others it begins at Christmas, the birth of Christ. In this book we begin our understanding of the Church Year with Advent.

There are six basic seasons to the Church Year.

1. **Advent**. Advent is a season of the four weeks preceding Christmas. For

years the world waited for the coming of a Messiah. To fully appreciate our long heritage, this dimension to our Christian faith, we observe the four weeks before Christmas Day as Advent.

2. **Christmas**. Christmas is a special holiday observed by almost every Christian group. As the early Christians looked back they saw that Jesus was the long awaited Messiah. His birth was a watershed of history. So, said the early Christians, we should certainly celebrate his birth. Many years had passed since Jesus was on earth, and no one knew his exact birth date. As so often has happened in the Christian experience, the Christians chose a date that was already a pagan celebration and just turned it into a Christian one. There was a Roman celebration called Saturnalia where gifts were exchanged. There was entertainment in homes and general merriment. Since Jesus was probably born sometime in the winter months, the date of the Saturnalia, December 25, was chosen to celebrate the birth of Jesus. Though we think of Christmas as a day, it is actually a season of fourteen days.

3. **Epiphany**. Wedged between Christmas and Lent is the little season of Epiphany. This season celebrates the coming of the Wisemen, the baptism of Jesus, the stories where Christ began to manifest himself to the world. It is often a season of outreach and mission emphasis in the church.

4. **Lent**. The season of Lent follows Epiphany. Early Christians had long celebrated the resurrection of Christ. As time passed they felt a need to prepare themselves spiritually for the Easter event. They remembered how Jesus spent forty days in the wilderness before he began his ministry. The season began with forty hours before Easter but grew to the forty days (not counting Sundays) before Easter.

5. **Easter**. Easter celebrates the resurrection of Christ and is the core and apex of our faith. History tells us it was the first special day celebrated by Christians. Just as in our own lives there are special days like birthdays and anniversaries, the day of resurrection is a special Christian festival around the world and becomes the high point in the entire Church Year. Easter falls on the first Sunday after the first full moon on or after March 21. It can occur as early as March 22 or as late as April 25. It is called a movable feast.

6. **Pentecost**. Completing the circle of the Church Year is the season of Pentecost. This season celebrates the coming of the Holy Spirit and covers a long period of calendar time. Just as the concept of the Church Year has evolved over centuries, this season seems to be still in flux. Some churches insert another season here: Kingdomtide, or Trinity, or Ordinary Time. This makes us aware that the Church Year as a vehicle for telling our faith story is alive and still forming. For educational purposes in this book we will deal with Pentecost as the entire season.

Because we remember something better if we set it to a rhythm and a melody, let's reinforce our learning of the six seasons of the Church Year by singing these words to the tune of "Joy, Joy, Joy, Joy Down in my Heart."

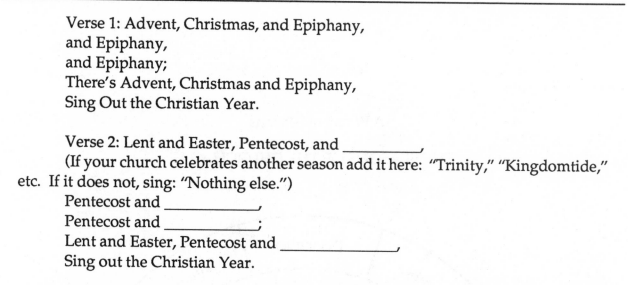

Verse 1: Advent, Christmas, and Epiphany,
and Epiphany,
and Epiphany;
There's Advent, Christmas and Epiphany,
Sing Out the Christian Year.

Verse 2: Lent and Easter, Pentecost, and _____,
(If your church celebrates another season add it here: "Trinity," "Kingdomtide,"
etc. If it does not, sing: "Nothing else.")
Pentecost and _____,
Pentecost and _____;
Lent and Easter, Pentecost and _____,
Sing out the Christian Year.

This concept of the Church Year has evolved through many ages and many lands and many branches of the church. It grew out of Jewish concepts of worship. The ancient Jewish calendar was a yearly round of festivals and holy days to tell the story of faith year after year. Christianity focuses the Church Year on the life of Christ and on telling and acting out the story of God's past actions so that we can see God's wonders in our lives today and have hope for the future. The Church Year has grown and is still growing, and this speaks to its essential catholicity. This simple framework of six seasons can be used in Christian education without losing any special denominational value or without departing from the New Testament faith. It has the value of becoming a point of compatible contact between the evangelical spirit and catholic churchmanship.

A second value is that this rhythm and flow of the seasons can be a source of energy for us as Christian educators. Sometimes in the church and church school, we feel we must always be on a high. We must jump from one celebration to another. Following the rhythm of the Church Year is a much more reasonable approach. For example, we turn inward for reflective spiritual growth during Lent and Advent and focus all our energies and ideas on outward festival celebration at Easter. We use different talents at different times. We can also teach that our lives, like the Church Year, turn inward and outward, have moments of high celebration and moments of dark groping. We do not reach a plateau and remain there; we find meaning and purpose in our own fluctuations.

You may want to study in more depth and detail how the concept of these seasons of the Church Year evolved. *Handbook of the Christian Year* (Abingdon Press, 1986) is one among several good books on this subject. For our purposes we are seeking an overview, a speaking acquaintance with the seasons of the Church Year.

"Calends" comes from the Latin word meaning "to proclaim." This word has given us the word "calendar."

Let's look now at the Church Year calendar in relation to our monthly calendar.

A Wheel of Seasons

THE SEASONS OF THE CHURCH YEAR

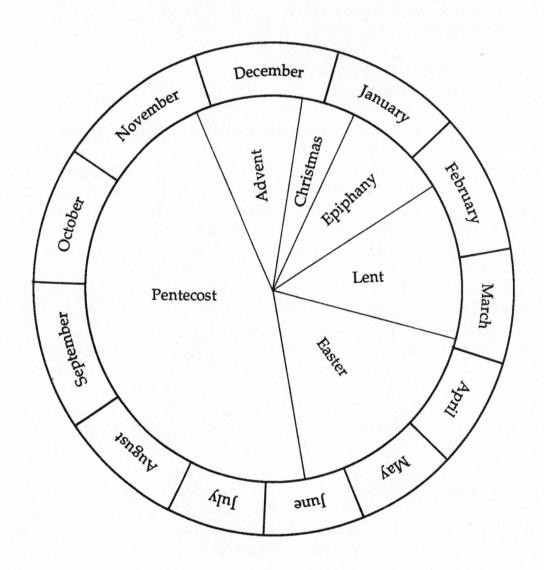

What Story Does the Church Year Tell?

John Westerhoff tells us that our identity is dependent on having a story that tells us who we are. Our understanding of life's meaning and purpose is dependent on having a story that tells us what the world is like and where we are going.

At the heart of the Church Year is the scriptural story that is entered into and perceived as happening again and again in the lives of the people today. We read and reread our stories. We read for meaning. Then we read again, for feeling.

The Church Year gives us a way to organize these Bible stories. It is through stories that our traditions and history and vision of life are shaped.

Let's affirm together that the stories of the Church Year are also our stories.

1. **The group** practices the hymn [chorus only], "Blessed Assurance."

> This is my story, this is my song,
> praising my Savior all the day long;
> This is my story, this is my song,
> praising my Savior all the day long.

2. **The leader** passes out six cards. If students are willing to stand and read they take a card. On these cards are some reminders of the biblical stories each season celebrates. After the reading of each card the group affirms that they are *our* stories by singing "Blessed Assurance" which they have just practiced.

Card 1:

The road to Bethlehem is a long, long road. For many years people had waited for a Savior to be born. Our ancestors Abraham and Sarah lived about 2,000 B.C. They left their home in the Arabian desert, walking to the promised land, waiting for a Savior.
Our ancestor Jacob gave the name "Israel" to the Hebrew nation. He was waiting for a Savior.
Our ancestor Joseph, doing his best in a strange land, was waiting for a Savior.
Moses, given the law but waiting for truth and grace, was waiting for a Savior.
David brought the ten commandments to Jerusalem and reigned forty years, waiting for a Savior.
Isaiah tried to lead the people back to the ways of righteousness by dreaming, teaching, preaching, waiting for a Savior.
We remember them during the season of Advent.

[All Sing "Blessed Assurance"]

Card 2:

In the fullness of time God did send a Savior. A child was born in Bethlehem who would show the world how to live. He would show us what God is really like. He was the light shining through the many years of dark waiting. And angels sang and stars shone and shepherds hurried to see. We remember these images during Christmas.

[All sing "Blessed Assurance"]

Card 3:
Events occurred that caused us to look at this baby in a new way. Strange and wonderful Magi came to worship him. The child developed into a unique man. A dove descended during his baptism. A water pot poured wine during a wedding. He gathered special disciples around him. He was getting ready to reveal himself to the world. We remember these stories during Epiphany.

[All sing "Blessed Assurance"]

Card 4:
Jesus went alone into the wilderness. The mountains were stark, slate-gray, and without vegetation. One rise of land dissolved into another. It was easy to get lost and confused. Jesus wandered about for forty days. Here he wrestled with temptations. We remember this time at Lent.

[All sing "Blessed Assurance"]

Card 5:
On a glorious spring morning, after a week of trials, tortures, suffering and death Jesus burst from his grave—resurrected! The stone guarding the entrance was rolled away. Soldiers fell, trembling, to their knees. Glowing angels appeared. Disciples ran with joyful news. We remember these stories at Easter.

[All sing "Blessed Assurance"]

Card 6:
Fifty days after Easter the disciples were gathered together in an upper room. They were a silent, fearful, dejected group, whispering, praying. Suddenly the Holy Spirit descended on them with rustling winds and tongues of fire. We remember this story at Pentecost.

[All sing "Blessed Assurance"]

Leader: So the seasons of the Church Year help us recall and celebrate important events in the life of Jesus and the church. We gather and tell our stories. No matter that they are the same stories we heard last year. Or, rather, it *does* matter that they are the same stories. When your families gather, don't they tell the same anecdotes year after year? The repeated narrative grows roots that give anchor in the storms of life and produce fruit that nourishes the soul. Repeating and repeating the stories of our faith deepens their meaning for us. We see pattern and purpose in the seasons of our lives and in the seasons of the Church Year.

Feeling the Seasons

(Using Games, Movement, and Music)

We have a basic understanding now of the stories the Church Year tells, of how the Church Year follows the life of Christ. Next our concern is to make the stories come alive for us. These are not just stories but *sacred* stories. They are stories that have multiple layers of meaning, stories that speak to us in different ways at different times of our lives, stories that cannot be interpreted in one single way. A sacred story is dead when the sacred is no longer heard through it, when it does not point us to God.

In this section we invite a joyful and serious participation in the stories. We are seeking to experience the feeling level of the stories.

There will certainly be times to study scripture and doctrine in the traditional sense of the word, but our purpose here is the experiential meaning of the story. We are not attempting to contemplate a story but to play it.

When we think of play, we often think of games. Games have the ability to transport us to a feeling level. The feelings we are seeking are delight, fun, freedom, and a particular feeling associated with the season. A kind of learning takes place in these play elements. Games, as well as being a way to sensitize and teach, can tell us a lot about the way our students view life. Attitudes and behavior in play weave a picture of who we are.

1. **Advent picks up the theme of waiting**. Let's play "Stand a Minute."

Stand a Minute

All students are instructed to rise and stand for *exactly* one minute, then sit down. Leader times the game with a stopwatch. When leader says "Go" the students stand and wait. Be sure there are no watches or clocks in sight. Leader tries to distract the students by talking to them or singing or walking among them.

The leader notes carefully on the time clock when the first person sits down, and who sits down on exactly one minute. The leader does not call time until the last person sits down. You may find students sit down as soon as fifteen seconds and remain standing as long as two minutes.

Leader announces results.

The group plays the game again. This time the leader is quiet and students may try tricks such as counting or feeling their pulse or anything they think will help.

Do they have a better feel for time?

But Advent is more than just waiting. It is waiting with anticipation and hope. Let's play again.

Wink-Um

Chairs are arranged in a circle with one empty chair. Girls sit in the chairs. A boy stands behind each chair, including the empty one. Girls sit on the edge of their seats. Boys have their hands behind their backs. The boy behind the empty chair looks around the circle and winks at a girl of his choice. This girl must run to the empty chair before the boy behind her tags her on the shoulder. If the girl is tagged, she remains where she is. If not, the boy who now has the empty chair does the winking. After a while, change and let the girls do the winking.

Many games with a "watch and wait" theme may be appropriate to catch the feeling level of this season.

2. **Christmas picks up feelings of joy, possibilities, and birth.** Let's sing "Go Tell It on the Mountain."

Group stands and sings the chorus with motions.

Song	Motion
Go, tell it on the mountain,	{Group makes climbing motions, pumping arms and lifting knees.}
Over the hills and everywhere,	{Join hands with person on each side and swing arms.}
Go, tell it on the mountain	{Climbing motions again.}
That Jesus Christ is born.*	{Hands to mouth in shouting posture.}

Add other verses and motions.

Christmas celebrates with joy everyone's birth. Play "Jump Your Name."

Jump Your Name

Group stands in circles of not more than eight persons. Going around the circle each person tells his or her first name and the entire group jumps the name. Jump on two feet for each consonant. Jump on one foot for each vowel. Jump and kick for each "y".

"Joy to the World"

Bring in rhythm instruments and play "Joy to the World."
First verse: rhythm with drums, sticks, and tone blocks.

* Words by John W. Work

Second verse: add handbells, maracas, tambourines, triangles, and bells on your wrists and ankles.

Third verse: add kazoos.

Fourth verse: Line up two or four abreast and march around the room playing instruments.

If you want to get fancy, play the instruments in various ways—over your head, crisscrossed, behind your back, etc.

Turn to the person beside you: If you could change one thing in the world what would it be? What one thing do you want to learn in your life?

3. **Feelings of Epiphany are of secrets revealed,** the manifestation of the previously unannounced. Try this group activity.

Who Am I?

Divide into groups of four. The first group of four comes forward. Each member tells his or her first name. The entire group looks them over for a few minutes. Then the group of four leaves the room and sends back one member who is covered with a blanket. This person crawls on the floor, snorts, groans, makes any kind of noise. The entire group guesses which of the four it is. They have only one guess so there must be group agreement. Each group of four has a turn.

Who Is Knocking?

Nine persons are chosen from the larger group. These persons go out of the room and draw a slip of paper telling who they are. The nine names are:

Police officer at night
Telegram deliverer
Rejected sweetheart
Messenger from the king
Gangster entering a hideaway
A spy
A frightened neighbor
Very young child
An old man

These same names are written on the board or newsprint for the entire group to see. Read the list to the larger group.

The nine persons one at a time knock on the door. Just by the way they knock, the larger group must guess who they are.

Those correctly guessed enter the room. The game continues until all are recognized.

Another Epiphany game would be for each participant to bring in a baby picture.

Pictures are mixed up. The entire group tries to match the baby picture with the current person.

4. **The feelings of Lent are bearing burdens**, engaging in struggle, enduring sacrifices.

Tug-of-War

The group is divided into two teams. A long rope is stretched out on a level surface. One team grabs one end of the rope; those on the other team, the other end. A handkerchief is tied in the exact middle of the rope. A line is drawn on the floor marking the middle. On "Go" the teams pull for thirty seconds. At the end of that time the team which has pulled the handkerchief on its side of the line wins.

Human Obstacle Relay

Divide the group into two teams. Station four persons in line before each team between the starting point and the turning point. The first person stands erect, the second with feet wide apart, the third in leapfrog position, the fourth erect. At the signal the first player on each team runs the course, running around the first player, diving through the legs of the second player, vaulting over the third and running completely around the fourth and returns direct to the starting line, touching off the second player who repeats the run.

Discuss: What is the hardest thing you have to do in your life? How do you sacrifice for others? How do others sacrifice for you?

5. **The feelings of Easter are great festivity**, order out of chaos.

Human Knot

Students stand in a circle. Each student joins hands with two more students who are not standing directly beside them. The students reach over and around to grasp the hands of others. When all are ready have them try to untangle the mess. Students can step over, duck under, step around to unravel the tangle, but they must not let go of hands. The game ends with everyone again standing in a circle. Order out of chaos!

Caterpillar and Butterfly Relay

Divide the group into teams. Line up in teams one behind the other facing the starting line. Establish a turning point some forty feet distant. Each player bends down and grasps the ankles of the player in front. The person at the head of the line places his hands on the floor and walks on hands and feet the entire time. At the signal, the entire line moves forward to the turning line, swings around and returns to the starting line. When the entire team, intact, has recrossed the finish line the last person will now be at the front of the line. Standing erect and turning around, the team is now ready for the butterfly part of the relay.

The first two persons in line stand abreast, linking inside arms around each other's waist. The outside arms flap like butterfly wings. In this position the two run together to the turning point, turn around, and flap back to their team. The next two persons do the same until the entire team has finished.

The winning team must complete both sections of the relay first.

Story Parts

The Easter story is read to the entire group (Mark 16:1-8). Divide the large group into groups of four. The small group has fifteen minutes to make a collage using old newspapers and magazines illustrating the story with words and pictures that express feelings.

At the end of this time the collages are shared and put together to form a huge collage.

6. **Pentecost reveals feelings of renewal** of God's people, coming alive to God's power.

Balloon Release

Students gather in a large open space.

Each student blows up a balloon, holding it by the neck. On the signal the students throw the balloons into the air. There is a wild zooming and dipping of released balloons.

Name Four

The group is seated in a circle. A ball or other object is passed around the circle to music. When the music stops the leader calls out a church category such as: church school teachers, church committees, church staff, church rooms, church missions, church ushers, church symbols. The player who has the ball when the music stops must name four examples in that category before the ball can go around the circle again.

I Am the Church

Everyone chooses a partner and stands facing him/her. During the chorus of the song "We Are the Church" partner acts out motions:

I am the Church	(Point to yourself)
You are the Church	(Point to your partner)
We are the Church together	(Partners shake hands)
All who follow Jesus	(Hands make circle over head)
All around the world	(Turn around)
Yes—We're the Church together	(Partners link arms)

During the verse of the song, partners scatter and find new partners in time to do the motions again to the next chorus. Sing many verses. No one may have the same partner twice.

Discuss: How did you get involved in the Church?

Modern Moods and Ancient Seasons

(Mix and Match)

In this movement of our time together, we want to think about how the Church Year and the Bible stories relate to our own lives here and now. How do modern moods and ancient seasons connect?

Though there is a historical significance to these feasts and festivals there is also a contemporary application for persons and for the faith community. And this is where the calendar comes into focus with power.

With this in mind let's look now at the seasons of the Church Year as they apply to our own lives today.

Instructions: Move into groups of six. Each group will have two envelopes. In each envelope there will be six slips of paper. One envelope has colored sheets, one white sheets. Each person is to draw a slip from each envelope. The colored slips are the season of the Church Year which we celebrate from the past, and the white slips are what we experience in the present.

Colored slips:

Advent
We recall how our people waited for the coming of the Messiah.

Christmas
We recall the birth of Jesus in Bethlehem.

Epiphany
We recall how Jesus revealed himself to the world.

Lent
We recall Jesus' forty days in the wilderness and his temptations.

Easter
We proclaim Jesus' resurrection.

Pentecost
We dramatize in word, act, and symbol the Apostles' receiving the gift of the Holy Spirit.

White slips:

> We express our dreams and hopes for this life and for life at the Second Coming.

> We celebrate all those times of new birth that have come into our own lives.

> We realize our responsibility to reveal or manifest Christ's love and power to the world. We recognize our calling as disciples. We get in touch with our own mission.

> This is a time to be in touch with our own "wilderness wandering" as we prepare for new risen life in Christ.

> We proclaim our own hope in the resurrection and our hope for loved ones who have died.

> We acknowledge and celebrate the Holy Spirit who comes to us.

When all have drawn two slips, the group puts the correct pieces together—the colored slips (Church Year season) and the corresponding white sheet (personal experience). All in the group must agree about the matching.

If there is more than one group, the groups come together and compare answers. When this is completed the teacher says, "From birth to death, joy to mourning, the story of the church supports us and directs us into a deeper experience of life made known through Christ."

Obviously, we do not experience new life just at Christmas; yet the church sets aside these special seasons to celebrate and to make holy all the times in our lives when we do experience these feelings. Thus, the Church Year takes every aspect of what it means to be alive and proclaims it holy. That's the excitement of the Church Year.

Picking up the great themes is what makes the difference between ineffective holiday celebrations and meaningful ones. We see how these same themes pulse through our lives, and our individual little stories are given meaning by the big story. The Church Year provides us with a structure in which we tell the story of Jesus and of the people of God again and again.

The good news of the Church Year is that God understands our human struggle and is with us at every stage of the journey. All of our small, personal stories touch on this greater story, and our lives are seen as holy. The holy is the ultimate source of meaning and we begin to move away from the unreality of a meaningless life.

Teacher: Now I'd like to ask you to ponder for yourself: Where are you now in your own life? Are you in an Advent period, getting ready, waiting? Are you in Christmas, experiencing something brand new?

Are you in a Lenten period, pondering your next step?

Maybe you are a combination.

Turn to the person beside you and share a seasonal moment. It may be either where you are now or a time when your personal life clearly reflected a seasonal theme.

Teacher: For our final activity, persons from the same church will get together (if more than one church is represented at your workshop). As a group decide where your church is in the Seasonal Cycle.

The group working together creates a paper sculpture using tissue paper. (Piles of tissue paper in the following colors are on a nearby table: purple, blue, white, green, black, white, yellow, and red.)

This sculpture is your group's attempt to express where your church is in the Church Year cycle. For example if your church is building, it may be Advent. If the feeling is of great activity, it may be Pentecost. If something new is emerging, it may be Christmas. Again, you may decide it is a combination.

Each person contributes some piece of paper to the final sculpture.

If there are more than one sculpture take time to see each of them.

Closing: All persons come together and sing "All the Way My Savior Leads Me."

If You Have Additional Time

Divide the large group into four small groups:
1. Advent/Christmas
2. Epiphany
3. Lent/Easter
4. Pentecost

Each group has five tasks:
1. Choose three traditions of the season. Act out in pantomime for the rest to guess.
2. Create a costume from old newspapers. Dress for your season.
3. Suggest three foods that would be appropriate for your season.
4. Lead the entire group in three songs or hymns for your season.
5. Create a symbol for your season.

When all have completed their assignment the entire group comes together to share.

A Workshop: Putting the Ideas to Work

The Church Year requires education and promotion before it can become effective. Following is a suggested outline for a two session workshop in which to learn about the Church Year, using the material previously presented.

Session I

What is the Church Year, and what is the story it tells?

Step 1: Leader presents the information in the section "What is the Church Year?"
Step 2: Students reinforce the learning by singing "Sing Out the Christian Year."
Step 3: Each student is given a copy of "Wheel of Church Seasons" for study and comment.
Step 4: Leader gives introduction and hands out six cards on the Church Year stories. Students stand and read sequentially, interspersed with group singing of "Blessed Assurance." [Chorus only]
Step 5: Close with group singing: "Tell Me the Stories of Jesus."

Session 2

What are the feeling levels of the seasons, and what are our personal connections with the seasonal themes?

Step 1: Look over the information in "Understanding the feeling level" and choose at least one activity for each season.
Step 2: Experience these with the group.
Step 3: Connect our personal story with the Bible story by matching slips of paper.
Step 4: Discuss the seasons in terms of our personal experiences.
Step 5: Sing "All the Way My Savior Leads Me."
Step 6: Where am I in the Church Year? Discussion.
Step 7: Where is my local church in the Church Year? Create a paper sculpture.

Extra Time Activity

1. Divide into four groups (Advent/Christmas, Epiphany, Lent/Easter, Pentecost).
2. Assign five tasks to each group.
3. All groups share.

Connections

Once we understand what the Church Year is, how can we incorporate it into the ongoing educational program of our church? What are its values for us?

The traditional classroom method of teaching still remains important for us. Basic Bible skills are necessary, for the Bible is the primary source of our story. We need to open the book and learn how to find and use what is in it.

The hymn book and worship tradition of our particular denomination are taught so that persons know their heritage and feel a part of their church community. There will still be the studying of how to apply the biblical learnings to the present moment. There will be studying of how political and social realities relate to our lives today and how we shape our Christian response to the issues that make headlines. There will still be the shaping of values and tracing of our particular denomination's roots. Graded courses using our church's curricula will still be the basis for most of our teaching.

But undergirding the study is the experience of the story. A value of the Church Year for us as educators is that we can celebrate Christ's story with more than the traditional teaching in the classroom. We can dramatize and sing and be storytellers and put ourselves into the story in a festive, joyful way.

The celebration of the Church Year can enliven children's imaginations, and inform and direct youth and adults. Generations can share the story together on trips and in fellowship halls, and outdoors, creating art and music together. Children and adults become intimately involved in the story. We are not watching, listening, or waiting; we are doing.

If our church worship is becoming more liturgical, experiences in the classroom centering around the stories the Church Year tells can help bridge the gap in what otherwise might be a meaningless worship liturgy.

In our church school, we experience the scriptural story and realize Christ is born anew in us here and now. We concentrate in the educational setting on experiencing not the church calendar but the gospel within the church calendar. We use its great themes to focus our feelings, but we remember that Christ preceded the church. The church produced the Bible, and the church produced the calendar to teach the Bible. We keep our priorities.

The following sections of the book will suggest ways to experience the seasons, the themes and the feelings of the Church Year.

We can divide the six seasons of the Church Year into two cycles: Christmas and Easter. The Christmas Cycle (Advent/Christmas/Epiphany) focuses around a fixed time, Christmas Day, December 25. The Easter Cycle (Lent/Easter/Pentecost) focuses on the movable date of Easter Day.

Our personal lives vibrate between these two great cycles. We come forth out of the darkness of birth and vanish into the darkness of death. How can looking at the Church Year themes help us to accept our life, live it, and proclaim it good?

THE CHRISTMAS CYCLE

(Advent, Christmas, and Epiphany)

If we follow the themes of the Church Year in our church schools for the Christmas cycle, what will be different?

First, we are more concerned with the heart of the season than the trappings. We, as church school teachers, must be in tune with the feeling level the season suggests, and our sensitivity will help create the ambiance. We seek integrity in our celebrations and their capacity for meaning.

Look at the three seasons that deal with the birth of Christ: Advent, Christmas, and Epiphany—the Christmas cycle.

The gospel story is always the center of all we do, but the authenticity of our teaching will come through if we keep in touch with our own felt feelings unearthed by the stories. Christmas is a deep, raw, honest sensing of human life as it is in God's eyes. We celebrate Christmas when something new is born here and now.

There is something within many of us that revolts against Advent and Christmas as we now experience it in our modern world with all its busyness and commercialism. Yet we seem unable to break its chains. Something deep within us feels it is wrong. Looking at the Church Year may help free us. What are the themes for this portion of the Church Year? How can we experience them in our classroom setting?

Let's explore four ideas, rich in feeling, that run through this Christmas cycle.

1. Quality of waiting
2. The hope of light from darkness
3. The yearning for God, the coming day of the Lord
4. The tenderness and mystery of birth

How do we bring these lofty ideas to our ordinary setting? It is here they must live or not at all.

There are times we want to share the story for the sake of the story. At other times, the reading launches a study of the concept. Always we seek to get in touch with the feeling.

Experiencing the Shepherds' Story

One method of teaching is to create an experience for the class. An experience is an honest thing. An experience does not try to deceive you. It just is, and we draw our own conclusions. I think our children, particularly in the "sit back and entertain me" environment created by television, are starved for experiences. The aim of this kind of teaching is not successful transmission of information, dates, or formulas. Rather, the aim is to enable participants to take part and feel. Faith, if it is to make any sense at all, must be experienced. Not what I've read about, seen on television, or been told, but what touches me personally. An experience touches us personally.

The following idea can be used for an intergenerational church experience or as an experience for an elementary church school class. The experience involves a twilight field trip to a farm or stable. Although this is not possible in all of our church situations, with a little scouting around could be a possibility for many.

The group visits a stable or barn and sits around a bonfire afterwards. In preparing for this experience the teacher should talk and explain before time the mood and atmosphere the class will be seeking to experience. Watching, looking, and listening we will approach the barn. Quietly and gently we will observe. Softly we will walk. Movement throughout the whole experience will be slow. The teacher will want to get an agreement from the class (verbally or by show of hands) that there will be no tricks or fooling around.

Though we often associate eating with a bonfire, try to save this experience until on the way home. Let the shepherd experience be one of quietness, awe, and receptivity.

Plan the trip so that transportation to the site allows you some time to approach the barn setting on foot. Walk quietly up a path, absorbing the sounds and smells and general atmosphere of animals preparing to retire for the night. If the teacher desires, he/she may offer suggestions to the class: Step softly. Watch gently. Put yourself into the scene. Touch the rough textures of straw. Feel the unhewed wood. Observe a trough or manger. Look around at overhead beams. Notice insect life. Become a part of this background. Gently touch fur and hide and feather.

The teacher should point out other items slowly and unobtrusively. It is important not to over-prescribe the students' experience with too many leading suggestions.

After a time, the teacher leads the class out.

Beyond the barn setting, in an open field or area if possible, gather around a bonfire. The teacher offers suggestions: Watch and feel the approach of darkness and the coming of stars. Wrap a cloak or blanket around you. Feel its rough texture.

After all are settled someone reads the shepherd story, Luke 2:8-20. In the silence that follows the reading, the teacher offers some suggestions for meditation: Feel the chill in the air. Watch the stars come out. Compare their brightness. Just participate in a silence shared here by family and friends and faithful people being present to one another.

After a time the teacher says: Now imagine yourself on a hillside in Bethlehem. Try to imagine being a shepherd.

Sing some shepherd songs together. "In Bethlehem Neath Starlit Skies" could be sung by a leader with everyone joining in the refrain, "Alleluia, Alleluia."

Other shepherd carols are "The First Noel," "While Shepherds Watched Their Flocks by Night," and "Away in a Manger." Since most classes know at least the first verse of these songs, there is no need to hand around songbooks.

Continue enjoying the bonfire mood.

Here the teacher may lead in discussing patience with the class with such questions as:

1. What do you think patience means?
2. How did the animals we saw show patience?
3. How would life be different if we never had to wait?
4. Why do you think waiting is meant to be a part of life?
5. Do you think that the older you get the more patient you become?

Before leaving all stand around the bonfire, join hands, and do a shepherd dance. To the tune of "Merrily We Roll Along" everyone skips to the right, singing:

> The little lambs are skipping, skipping,
> Skipping, skipping,
> Skipping, skipping,
> The little lambs are skipping, skipping
> All on Christmas night.

(All persons circle to left with short, running steps, singing:)

> Shepherds all are running, running,
> Running, running,
> Running, running,
> Shepherds all are running, running
> All on Christmas night.

(All raise joined hands to center and sing:)

> All of us are coming, coming,
> Coming, coming,
> Coming, coming,
> All of us are coming, coming
> All on Christmas night.

With the group still holding hands, the teacher says: The shepherds' faith reminds us that God has not abandoned the world. The shepherds didn't argue. They just said, "Let's go and see." Where there is love there are always miracles. Many miracles rest not on power from far off, but on our looking closer so that, for a moment, our eyes can see and our ears can hear what is here about us always. Let us pray that our ears may become sensitive to angels singing and our eyes to miracles around us.

The teacher or leader will set the tone for this experience. It seems that sometimes in Christian education, we have the curious teaching habit of making what we read and study more real than what we see and experience. But in truth, we are what we experience. Experiences form us. Experiential poverty is not uncommon even in wealthy and polished surroundings.

Open your class to a Christmas experience. Try to be open to the wonder and awe available to us in ordinary experiences.

An Art Festival of Light

Pick up the theme of "light out of darkness" which runs through the whole Christmas cycle (the Light is coming, the Light is here, the Light is revealed) by having the entire church school take part in an Art Festival of Lights.

Each church school class—from toddlers through adult—would create a special Light Display in their room. Over a period of weeks, the entire church school would be transformed into a variety of learning areas. Creativity would be encouraged. John 1:5 would be the scripture they would attempt to interpret: The light shines in the darkness and the darkness has never put it out.

The display could simply be pictures of light drawn by young children on construction paper and put on the wall. Brainstorm with your class and let the creative ideas flow.

Here are some more suggestions to share with your classes, but remember your situation is unique and the creative potential of your class taps different talents and abilities.

- Youth might want to create a display with fluorescent lights and incandescent lights and strobe lights.
- A single bare tree branch decorated with small white Christmas lights could be used in one room.
- If there are artists in your church or community, display their works in halls and narthex, and observe their use of light.
- Those classes which are more craft-minded could make small clay lamps with self-hardening clay. First, shape a hollowed out bowl to hold vegetable or corn oil. Make a lip on the edge of the bowl to hold the dry end of a wick, coiled up in the oil. Line your window ledges, furniture tops, and shelves with these small burning lamps. Glasses of colored water in front of the lamps create the image of the twinkling of a million stars.
- The glow of candles might be one class's choice of Light—all shapes, all sizes, all colors. They might chose to make their own candles.

- Starlight could be the theme of one class. Cover posterboard in star shape with foil and hang on walls, from ceiling, and in windows.
- A Moravian Star might be the choice of another class.
- One class might create a tunnel effect with light at the end of the tunnel.
- A class could write poetry on light. Use this phrase to begin and have students complete it: "Come soon! Everything is waiting for light" or "Come soon! It's a matter of life and death."
- A light montage is a possibility. Have students find pictures in magazines showing the many uses of light.
- Your Light Festival might include one room for persons who have light objects as a hobby. For example, someone might collect old kerosene lamps.
- If you are within distance of a museum, investigate exhibits on loan pertaining to light.

These are only meant to be thought starters. Begin with these, but look to your own church school for ideas and talents. Your Lights Art Festival can become an all-church event.

An important part of the festival is the closing.

On a designated day during the church school hour, visit the other classrooms. Have music playing (for example, the hymn "Walk in the Light"). Have a printed program with names of teachers and grade level and short description of classroom display written by the class.

You might prefer to visit the other classrooms on an evening when the lights will be more appreciated.

Have a period of free visitation, then at a designated time all gather, give everyone a small candle. When these are lit, a leader leads the entire group outside, single file, around in circles and spirals, and finally into one large circle , singing "This Little Light of Mine." End in the parking lot. Car lights may also be turned on.

Leader: As we watch our candles burn and our lights flicker, we see a symbol of love which dipped a spirit into human form, that the world in its darkness might be made more beautiful.

From different spots around the circle, two persons read out the following Scripture on light.

Reader 1: The people who walked in darkness have seen a great light. They lived in a land of shadows but now light is shining on them.

Isaiah 9:2 , TEV

Reader 2: The Word was the source of life and this life brought light to mankind. The light shines in the darkness and the darkness has never put it out.

John 1:4-5, TEV

A Litany

All: Jesus Christ is the Light of the World.

Men: The light no darkness can overcome.

Women: Arise, shine for your light has come.

Children: Let us share Christ's light with others.

Leader: Christians, regardless of age, are called to bring the light of God into their world. The Son of God will (has) come. Darkness recedes. In worship, prayer, and thanksgiving, we prepare ourselves. Light and Love will reign.

Closing Response (all sing) Send out your light and your truth; let them lead me (Psalm 43:3).

The images of light feed our imagination and have the power to deepen and sharpen the sense of God's presence. Light is a powerful symbol of Christ come into the world; his very life, luminous, lit by a fire from beyond the world. Incarnation is so hard to grasp: the Word, flesh, God, man. We experience light and try to understand.

A Rocking Baby

A third sweeping theme running through the Christmas cycle is the theme of birth and new life.

Birth touches the heart at its most tender part.

The Rocking Baby Ceremony celebrates this theme. It originated in Bledworth near Nottingham, England in medieval times and is still held there. This Christmas custom in its original form was a short play depicting the presenting of the baby Jesus at the Temple (Luke 2:22-38). Today, parents of the most recently born baby boy bring him to the church where he is rocked in a 100-year-old cradle decorated with flowers. The "rocking baby" as he is called, receives a Bible and his name is added to the official Register of Rocking.

We can pick up on this idea in a number of ways in our church school classrooms. The following program is suggested for pre-school children.

Have a cradle in the classroom of the pre-school children; they will enjoy relating to it. Let them take part in adding greenery and flowers and berries around the edge and sides of the cradle.

Flowers have long been associated with the birth of Jesus.

Have on hand for the decorating:

holly

poinsettias

white Christmas roses

rosemary

evergreens

As the class works together adding the flowers and greenery to the cradle, the teacher tells a legend that goes with each plant.

Begin with greenery (pine, fir, etc.): Evergreens remind us of God because they stay green and alive when all other plants look dead and bare. They remind us that spring will come.

Rosemary:

We notice rosemary's sweet smell and beautiful gray-green color.

> A legend says that once Mary hung the baby Jesus' clothes to dry on a rosemary bush. After that it always had this wonderful smell. It received its color from Mary's cloak which she threw on the branches.

Let's add rosemary to our cradle.

Poinsettia:

> One day a little peasant girl was standing by the doors of the church sadly watching all the people leave beautiful gifts at the statue of baby Jesus. She was sad because she had nothing to give. Finally she picked a big bunch of green-leafed plants that grew beside the road. The people were very cruel and laughed out loud to see the little girl in her tattered clothes taking a bunch of weeds as her offering. She was very ashamed and her face reddened. Then so did the plants. Its leaves turned into beautiful flowers. The people were amazed at this miracle and very sorry that they had laughed.

Holly:

> A legend says that the crown of thorn Christ wore before his death was made of holly leaves. When the crown pricked Christ's forehead his blood flowed over the holly berries, changing them from white to red. See the red berries of the holly?

White Christmas rose:

> Once a group of very poor people were driven farther and farther into the forest where, being not only poor but far from home, they could make nothing for their children for Christmas. But Christmas Eve night the silent forest gleamed with a whitish glow. The next morning the ground was covered with Christmas roses.

When the cradle is decorated the children dip their fingers in a bowl of water and sprinkle the flowers. As this is happening the teacher shares this legend:

> Long ago when Mary and Joseph and baby Jesus were fleeing to Egypt, they became very thirsty and dusty. In that country water was very

scarce. They had been on the road several days and badly needed water. Finally, they saw a small house. Joseph knocked on the door and asked if they might please have some water. The woman who answered the door told them she too had a baby, but he was ill and had a fever. She was just going to bathe the sick baby to cool his fever. It was all the water she had. Then the woman did a very kind thing. She said: You bathe baby Jesus first and afterwards I'll wash my baby in the same water. And so they did. But when the sick child washed his sores healed and his fever left. When the mother lifted him out of the water, the baby was healthier and happier than she'd ever seen him.

Holding a Bible, the teacher gathers the students around and tells the story of the presentation of Jesus:

When Jesus was forty days old, Mary and Joseph took him to the Temple to thank God that he was born. There was an old man named Simeon in the Temple. He had served God for many years and he longed to see the Savior whom God had promised to send into the world. When he saw Jesus he knew this was the special baby God had promised. He came eagerly to meet Mary, and she let him hold the baby. This made him very, very happy.

Another faithful servant of the Lord in the temple was Anna. When she saw baby Jesus she too gave thanks to God.

Teach the class the Bible verse:

How happy are those who live in your
Temple, always singing praise to you.
Psalm 84:4, TEV

Sing it with your class.

Let the class act out the story. One child can be Mary, one Joseph, another Simeon, another Anna. A simple scarf draped over their heads will help them get in character. Use a doll for baby Jesus. Designate a section of the room to be the Temple. Simeon and Anna stand here. Mary, carrying Jesus, and Joseph walk to the Temple. Let the children, in character, respond any way they wish.

Afterwards, the doll can be put in the decorated cradle and rocked.

On the same day or another day, you might walk with your class to your church nursery and see the babies there, or go as a class to visit the newest born baby in your congregation. There is mystery and miracle in every single human birth. A newborn baby calls out feelings within us, feelings of love and kindness and happiness. Very carefully, some of the children may hold the baby.

Tell your class that angels sang at the birth of Jesus and may sing at the birth of each child. What song did the angels sing when you were born? Sing "Away in a Manger" to the new baby.

Explain to your class that a blessing is a special wish for someone made before God. Ask each member of the class to give a blessing to the new baby. Write down these blessings and present them to the parents of the new baby.

Yearning for God

There is yet another profound feeling that the church addresses at this season of the year. Deep within us is a yearning for God. It is a kind of homesickness that nothing can ever satisfy. Sometimes we confuse this feeling with nostalgia or romance, but at its root it is a longing for God.

When we touch this feeling, we better understand Advent and the overtones of the Second Coming of Christ, which Advent also points to. Christ's birth was an actual, long-awaited event, but we still long to be reunited with God from whom we feel cut off.

If we can accept and help our students accept that the feeling of Advent (waiting and longing for God) is always with us perhaps we can truly celebrate the Season.

What can we do to make this feeling surface in the classroom setting?

We find expression of this longing in music, and some of our hymns of this season give voice to our feelings. In teaching hymns, we give our students some resources with which to express their feelings.

The words of "O Come, O Come Emmanuel," a familiar Advent hymn, reveals this longing. Sing it over and over with your class. The more familiar a song is to us, the more we like it. Sing it slowly and deliberately. Don't worry if children don't understand the words. In fact, this is an advantage. The sounds of the words can have their own meaning for the singers, can be an utterance of their longing. If you have some non-singers in your class, they can become an ostinato chorus who chant the words "come-come-come" as the rest of the class sings over them.

The American folk-hymn "Wayfaring Stranger" sung with guitar accompaniment also brings forth our deep feelings of alienation. As the feelings bubble up, we let our bodies sway in expression to the music.

Sometimes our students feel uncomfortable moving to music; yet when we are seeking to bring forth deep feelings this can be a powerful avenue.

Ephphatha Sunday

(Suggested for a young adult class with open space for movement)
An Advent scripture is Isaiah 35:5,6:

Then shall the eyes of the blind be opened.
The ears of the deaf shall be unstopped.

Then shall the lame man leap as an hart and
the tongue of the dumb shall sing. For in
the wilderness shall waters break out and
streams in the dessert.

(KJV)

The Aramaic word for "be opened" is "ephphathah." Your church school class might observe "Ephphatha Sunday." After reading the Scripture, ask your students to look at communicating through movement and other non-verbal means. Five experiences follow.

Teacher: From birth until death we are moving, always going somewhere, never at rest. What does all this movement tell us about ourselves?

Experience 1:
Begin with hands. Each student stands facing a partner. Students illustrate with their hands (no words) the following verbs.

Grab
Stroke
Scratch
Squeeze

Write them for the class to see. Students are seated and each discusses with his or her partner:

1. How did you feel as you did these actions? Could you understand each other?
2. Which action was easiest for you to do?
3. Which was the most pleasing action?
4. Which of these four actions best describes how you react to the world around you?
5. Try to think of persons who personify these actions in their approach to life.

Experience 2:
Stand again facing your partner. This time we will use movements with emotional content. Each student shows his or her partner the following idea with movement and body posture only:

Cringe
Threaten
Struggle
Hug

Allow time for the feeling of the posture to permeate.

Teacher: Often our body posture gives hints of body/mind/spirit inter-relatedness. Write the four words for the class to see.
Discuss with your partner:

1. Which of the movements was most tense for you?
2. Which most grasping?
3. Which most jerky?
4. With which did you feel most uncomfortable?
5. With which were you most comfortable?
6. Do you agree with the idea that our movements often reflect and reinforce our state of mind?

Experience 3:

Teacher: Our third experience uses movement to express ideas. This time work in groups of three persons. We will use our bodies to illustrate these ideas.

First, each person expresses the idea :

Escape
Search
Wither
Bloom

Allow time for the feeling of the body movement to permeate.

After this experience the three persons create an arm trio. Working together you attempt to find positions in which you can move your arms together to express the four ideas. Begin and end in stillness, framing your movements.

Discuss. Write the four words for the class to see.

1. Did you feel comfortable using your body to express ideas?
2. With which of the four did you feel most uncomfortable?
3. With which did you feel most comfortable?
4. How did you like working in trios?

Experience 4:

Much of Scripture uses body posture to describe relationships. God's relationship to humankind is described in Leviticus 26:11-12 "And I will set my tabernacle among you and my soul shall not abhor you. And I will *walk* among you and will be your God and you will be my people."

Group stands in a circle. Music to "Wayfaring Stranger" is played. Persons walk around the circle in time to the music, but each person finds his/her own stride with which they feel comfortable. Let moving feet and swinging arms express inner feelings. The stride that is right for you will be satisfying and relaxing. You will be synchronized with gravity and the terrain. Some feel more comfortable with longer strides. After a time some may move out of the conforming circle to freer space. Each moves at his/her own comfortable pace.

After experiencing this for a time ask the class to stand perfectly still during one verse of the song.

Discussion:

1. Idioms are sayings that have hidden meaning. The expressions do not mean exactly what words say. Think about our idiom "He took it all in stride" or "I have found my stride." Have you experienced what this means? Give an example.

This "walk," this stride, our "appointed course," is a familiar symbol in our spiritual life. It is for God to determine how long our journey will last and under what circumstances we shall finally reach our destination.

2. Stumbling is sometimes an experience when walking. Imagine the feeling of stumbling. What do we do after such an experience? Recall an actual experience. What were the consequences?

3. There is a dignity in standing. Think about our idiom: "Take a stand" "Stand up for what you believe" and "Be outstanding." Have you experienced what this means? Give an example.

Teacher: The possibility of intimate union with God lies hidden within the commonplace activity of walking, stumbling and standing.

Experience 5:

Teacher: To live is a moving balance and we do not always travel alone. Our bodies, can be instruments of praise to God, whether playing solo or in an orchestra.

Now the music shifts to the hymn "O Come, O Come, Emmanuel." The group stands in a tight circle.

Teacher: Native Americans say, "When people come together to have a circle, they speak from their hearts." We will speak now, without words, from our heart.

O Come, O Come, Emmanuel
  {Group reaches to each other, palms touching.}

And ransom captive Israel
  {Group interacts, wrists touching.}

Who mourns in lonely exile here
  {Group interacts, fingertips touching.}

Until the Son of God appears
  {Group interacts, elbows touching.}

Rejoice! Rejoice! Emmanuel
  {Group interacts, arms around shoulders.}

Shall come to Thee, O Israel.
  {Group joins hands, raises them overhead.}

Teacher: Our bodies can become simple, open, clear channels of the Spirit. We can relieve tensions that accumulate, sapping the subtle energy needed for the simple, clear presence of God's Spirit.

In this kind of movement—walking in stride using fluid, graceful movements with a steady, alert body—we become more observant. Our eyes are open, our ears unstopped. Hear again the words of Isaiah (35:5 and 6). What do the students think now of his poetic ways of expressing yearning for God?

Sensitizing

Perhaps our job in the church school in dealing with the theme of yearning for God is simply to bring the feeling out into the open, name it, identify it. There is a deep longing within us which no natural happiness will satisfy. Then give our students a way to express this yearning, through music, movement, and drama.

A youth class which has had experience in sensitizing activities and with a dramatic bent might respond to the following method of seeking to understand the feeling of yearning found in the Advent season. Do not try this activity unless your class has had experiences together focusing on feelings.

Step 1: Hold the students outside the classroom until all have assembled.

Step 2: Spray the room with perfume. Then lead your students into the room where delicate wisps of the scent remain. Ask the students to just smell. They sit in their regular seats.

Step 3: From outside the room play from a recording the closing notes of an obscure musical work, letting the tones drift away into silence. Instruct your class to listen.

Step 4: By prearrangement have a student burst into the room carrying a shred of newspaper and read dramatically: On Obser in outer space the spring season is just beginning. New purple growth is covering the landscape. Water ferns are unfolding. The giant Snagora beasts are hatching.

Step 5: The student leaves. Then the teacher says: The feeling of Advent is the scent of a flower we have not found, the echo of a tune we have not heard, news from a country we have never visited, looking at a door we have only seen from the outside.

Step 6: Follow this experience with an art activity.

Students will be asked to create a symbol of Advent. It may be one with which they are familiar or a new symbol catching up the feeling of yearning.

Have on hand these supplies:

    various lengths and colors of yarn

    bowl of liquid starch

    wax paper

    weighted items

Instructions: Give students time to create in their minds the symbol of their choice. When all are ready, students choose strips of yarn and dip them in the liquid starch. The pieces are arranged on a piece of wax paper in the Advent design. Cover with a second piece of wax paper and press under a weighted object. Let the yarn dry thoroughly, perhaps until the next week.

When the designs are dry, add an ornament hook to the stiff symbol and hang in your classroom for the remainder of the season.

Room Environment

What does our church school classroom look like during this cycle?

The traditional greens and candles and Nativity pictures and creches adjusted to the age level of our class will speak of the Christmas Season.

In addition you might like to try an idea from India to pick up the global consciousness this season encompasses.

Create Rangoli

In India the women use colored rice flour to prepare special designs called "rangoli" on the doorsteps and in their courtyards to welcome special guests. Pick up on this idea by designating a special corner of your classroom as a "Welcome Jesus" corner. Have your class, working together, create a design, then make this design on the floor with colored sand. Consider traditional Advent and Christmas symbols such as the Star of Bethlehem, Advent Rose, Christ monograms such as Chi Rho, Alpha and Omega with the letters IHS, a crown, or a shepherd's crook. Symbols suggest ideas for contemplation. If this creates a cleaning problem for your room, make your rangoli on construction paper. Draw the symbol with white glue. Sprinkle the colored sand over it. Then shake the remaining sand into a wastebasket. The sand will adhere to your glue design. These pieces of construction paper can then be put on the floor in your "Welcome Jesus" corner. What do we do with this symbol? What is expected is an act of contemplation. This is a sign that says: There is something more here.

Imagine Angels

Younger children might like the idea of surrounding their room with angels. Read to the class Luke 2:13(TEV): "Suddenly a great army of heavenly angels appeared."

Secure drawing paper in a long roll and stretch it around your room on the walls. Instruct your class members to draw angels anyway they like. In addition they might make angel sun-catcher for the classroom windows, bring in a collection of angels, or draw angels to dangle from the ceiling.

When art forms in decorations enter into religious education, the thoughts of the class may be directed in ways that may become a source of spiritual experience. Spiritual growth often happens in these subtle ways. Almost unknowingly, we absorb images to ponder.

How do we teach children that something is special? By the way adults react. Add to your classroom atmosphere a teacher's frame of mind of anticipation, contented joy, quiet happiness and awe in the presence of a miracle.

Christmas Music in the Classroom

Music is a crucial ingredient to the celebration of the Christmas cycle, and here I confess I have a problem with following the Church Year. Liturgical churches suggest we sing Advent songs during Advent, Christmas carols such as "Silent Night" only at Christmas, and "We Three Kings" at Epiphany. But at the feeling level, I want to sing the beloved Christmas carols all through Advent and Christmas, then stop as soon as Christmas Day is over.

Maybe I am indoctrinated by the secular world, but singing Christmas carols after Christmas Day seems as stale as used Christmas wrapping paper or an after-Christmas turkey carcass. And singing "O Come, All Ye Faithful" and "Joy to the World" only at Christmas is not enough.

Since I strongly believe music sets the tone for a season and is our most powerful means of expressing feelings, I have puzzled long and hard over my contradictory feelings about Christmas carols. Something deep within me wants to sing Christmas carols during Advent.

Here is the way I justify and rationalize my current feelings. When we sing Christmas carols, we are stirring up a lot of memories and associations. When we sing Christmas carols, I think we are making a ritual sound. In contrast to other hymns I sing, I don't think I dwell as much on the words or even the cadence and tone. I long to hear that ritual sound when Christmas comes around. Setting the mood with Christmas carols puts me right there *in* the experience—receptive for the greater themes the season proclaims.

Thus, in our church school classes, I recommend we sing any and all of our tremendous repertoire of Christmas carols. Let the ritual sounds ring out!

Following the Church Year through the Christmas cycle allows us to be creative, inventive, and imaginative. The Church Year has great themes that touch on deep, personal feelings as well as the great verities of the Christian faith. Following these, we will have little place in our church school for Santa Claus or commercial endeavors.

THE EASTER CYCLE

(Lent, Easter, Pentecost)

As we move to the Easter cycle of the Church Year (Lent/Easter/Pentecost), we touch the heart of our Christian faith: Jesus' suffering, death, and resurrection, which brings into focus God's whole history with mankind.

To many of us, Lent has the image of a formidable season, stressing the manifold sins and wickedness of humankind, the wrath and indignation of God against us. But Lent can be a season of hope and creativity. Lent has always been a teaching season, but, instead of emphasizing our sinful nature, we can examine our lives in the realm of gifts and graces. It is by God's gracious gift that we have life. During Lent we explore what we are doing with it.

We acknowledge our fallibility, our vulnerability, and our incompleteness, but we trust the human condition. Through Jesus and the mystery of his death and resurrection, we struggle to make sense out of the painful side of living. We affirm that God's purpose is being worked out. Forgiveness is important, but we don't wallow in our sinfulness. We accept it and move beyond. In penitence we seek to make whole again and repair the damage done.

This spirit of hope was captured for me in an incident I read about Elisabeth Kübler-Ross' visit to Mardanek, a Polish concentration camp. The camp had a sinister crematorium, and all the other indications of horror we associate with World War II and the Holocaust. Inside barracks which had been a pre-death holding room for many German Jews, and amid the graffiti which decorated the walls which had become their common tomb, Ross found children's drawings of butterflies, a traditional symbol of hope.

What more obvious sign of human wickedness than these concentration camps? Yet something expressed in the Easter cycle hurdles even this. We are redeemed. The divine spark in us is not completely extinguished. Blessing and hope conquer sin and wickedness. We go forth with courage. We embrace pain. We touch into our own suffering and the suffering of others, and the divine, creative nature transcends. Lent helps us in this period of moving through.

Then Easter itself comes, the Breakthrough, the Ecstatic Moment when we see beneath the surface of ordinary things. God took the worst of life and transformed it.

Through Pentecost we try to live out this transformation. We celebrate Pentecost wherever the Spirit is present, the promised comforter, the vivifying Presence.

Again, in the church school we seek to understand these seasons by getting in touch with the feeling level that both our Scriptures tell and our human lives experience.

What are some foundational themes?
1. Repentance and Reconciliation
2. Saving work of Christ and our participation in it
3. Renewal and commitment to the Lordship of Christ in our common life
4. God's overwhelming Easter victory
5. Coming of the Spirit

Ash Wednesday
A Service of Tears

Ash Wednesday marks the beginning of the Lenten season, the forty days of preparation for Easter. Coming in the middle of the week and an occasion of worship rather than study, this day is seldom observed in church school. Yet it seems a good thing to have a definite beginning to this season, an arresting service that causes us to be aware of a different mood and new beginnings in our faith. This marks a time for putting aside our failures and mistakes of the past. It is a day of readiness, of preparation.

Children need a sense of forgiveness as much as any adult. Children understand the feeling of being alienated from others by wrongdoing and need the steps of reconciliation. The assurance that God forgives and restores rather than judges is important in the development of a healthy spirituality.

This particular service is suggested for Ash Wednesday afternoon after school. Instead of the traditional symbol of ashes, we use a symbol expressive of forgiveness and repentance to children: tears.

Room setting: (As children enter, a tape of the African-American spiritual "Nobody Knows the Trouble I've Seen" is playing.)

At the front of the room is a cross. On the top bar of the cross is a symbol for the eye of God. Draw a simple eye, eliptical in shape with a pupil. Refer to a book on Christian symbols if necessary.

A table placed just inside the room contains colored cellophane paper cut into tear shapes of all sizes, and rolls of thin paper ribbon in a variety of colors.

Opening Activity: Children choose cellophane paper "tears," attach them to ribbons of color and with the help of a leader, attach the tear streamers to the arms of the cross at varying levels. There is a transparency to the slightly fluttering streamers like our own tears.

Introduction of theme and movement prayer: Children are seated in chairs in a semi-circle facing the cross with room between chairs for movement.

Leader: This is a solemn occasion, a time when we come to God with our tears and our sadness. God hears our weeping and is always with us. Just as the Eye of God is above our tears, God is always aware when we cry. God hears our sighs and counts our tears.

When we cry, we use our voices but also our bodies. Let's listen to the words from a psalm and try to experience the words with our bodies. Please stand by your chairs. Pretend your back is against a wall and in slow motion someone hits you in the stomach. Slowly drop your head forward, bend over. Your body should look like the letter "C." In this position, listen to these words from Psalm 142:6:

> Listen to my cry for help,
> For I am sunk in despair.

Have children repeat the words after you. Then, lead the class to movement, saying: Now slowly begin to straighten your body. Let your shoulders come back and your head lift.

> I call to the Lord for help,
> I plead with God.

(Children repeat words.)

Teacher: Now, raise your right hand above your head and look up, saying:

> I tell God all my troubles.

(Children repeat words.)

Teacher: Children, raise both hands high over your head. Then say:

> I plead with God.
> I bring God all my complaints.

(Children repeat words.)

Teacher: Now fold your hands in prayer and bow your head. Speak aloud:

> When I am ready to give up,
> God knows what I should do.

(Children repeat words.)

Teacher: Children, stand straight, hands open wide to the side, palms up.

Set me free from my distress,
I will praise you
Because of your goodness to me.

(Children repeat words.)

Teacher: Be seated.

Bible Story and Discussion

Teacher or leader: Hear the story of Jesus weeping over Jerusalem.

He came closer to the city and when
he saw it, he wept over it saying,
If you only knew today what is
needed for peace. But now you cannot see it.

Luke 19:41-2

Think of the last time you cried. Were you hurt physically? Did someone hurt your feelings? Were you losing something you wanted? Were you frightened? Did you dread something? Have you ever cried because of something you did wrong?

Tears are a way of saying "I'm sorry." Every one of us has done things for which we are sorry. None of us is as strong or as brave as we would like to be. God knows this and always forgives us.

Group Singing

"Kum Ba Yah" (with motions)

Kum Ba Yah (Come by Here)

1. Kum ba yah, my Lord, kum ba yah.

Kum ba yah, my Lord, kum ba yah.

Kum ba yah, my Lord, kum ba yah.

Oh, Lord, kum ba yah.

1 Kum ba yah, my Lord, kum ba yah.
Kum ba yah, my Lord, kum ba yah.
Kum ba yah, my Lord, kum ba yah.
Oh, Lord, kum ba yah!

2 Someone's praying, Lord, . . .

3 Someone's crying, Lord, . . .

4 Someone needs you, Lord, . . .

5 Someone's singing, Lord, . . .

6 Let us praise the Lord, . . .

WORDS AND MUSIC: Afro-American Spiritual, DESMOND, arr. by William Farley Smith
Arr. copyright © 1988 The United Methodist Publishing House.

It's Me, O Lord
(Standing in the Need of Prayer)

R It's me, it's me, it's me, O Lord,
   standing in the need of prayer.
   It's me, it's me, it's me, O Lord,
   standing in the need of prayer.

1 Not my brother, not my sister, but it's me, O Lord, . . .

2 Not the preacher, not the deacon, but it's me, O Lord, . . .

3 Not my father, not my mother, but it's me, O Lord, . . .

WORDS AND MUSIC: Afro-American Spiritual, PENITENT, arr. by William Farley Smith

Circle dance

All children stand in a large circle. They number off "one" and "two" around the circle.

Music to "It's Me, O Lord" is played on piano. Holding hands, children circle to the right singing:

> It's me, it's me, it's me, O Lord
> Standing in the need of prayer.

Now all circle to the left singing:

> It's me, it's me, it's me, O Lord
> Standing in the need of prayer.

Standing still in the circle, hands clasped, all number "ones" raise right hand holding partner's hand:

> Not my brother

All number "twos" raise right hand holding partner's hand:

> Not my sister

All swing hands up and back holding partner's hand.

> But it's me, O Lord,
> Standing in the need of prayer.

Repeat words and action.

> Class is seated.

Old Testament Scripture and Receiving Balm

Leader: We have told God about our tears. We have brought our tears to God. We have asked that God will forgive us and help us. In the Old Testament of our Scriptures, the prophet Jeremiah looked at the sorrows of the people and cried to God:

> Is there no balm in Gilead; is
> there no physician there? why then
> is not the health of the daughter
> of my people recovered?
>   Jeremiah 8:22 (KJV)

The dictionary defines "balm" as a lotion used for healing or relieving pain. A beautiful hymn tells us that the balm we seek is the love of Jesus.

Soloist or group sings: "There Is a Balm in Gilead." As he or she is singing, the leader brings a bowl of sweet-smelling hand lotion to the front. The children are instructed to come forward one at a time and hold out their hands, palms down. The leader draws a cross on their hands with the sweet-smelling lotion. They return to their seats.

There Is a Balm in Gilead

R There is a balm in Gilead
to make the wounded whole,
there is a balm in Gilead
to heal the sin sick soul.

1 Sometimes I feel discouraged,
and think my work's in vain.
But then the Holy Spirit
revives my soul again.

2 If you can't preach like Peter,
if you can't pray like Paul,
just tell the love of Jesus,
and say he died for all.

WORDS AND MUSIC: Afro-American Spiritual, BALM IN GILEAD, arr. by William Farley Smith

Arr. copyright © 1988 The United Methodist Publishing House.

Dismissal

Leader: Today marks a new beginning of faith for us. We have repented with tears and are free to grow by the grace of God. All sing the round "Go Now in Peace."

Go Now in Peace

May be sung as a round.

WORDS: Natalie Sleeth (Luke 2:29)
MUSIC: BETTY, Natalie Sleeth

Burden Bearers

There are no easy answers to pain and hurt. We wonder why we must suffer and bear heavy burdens. To give a pat answer would be to trivialize the experience. The following service attempts to give students an experience in this area. It is suggested for an evening youth meeting.

A burden bearer is a structure that is a common sight along many roads in India. It is made of two upright slabs of stone with another stone across the top, not unlike a smaller version of the Stonehenge structures. Also common along the roads in India is the sight of persons heavily laden with packs upon their backs and heads. The burden-bearer structure is built and of such a height so that persons may rest the burdens they carry upon the cross stones without the difficulty of setting their burden on the ground then lifting it up again. For Christians in India the burden bearer has become a symbol of Christ.

Opening Activities

The first activity is the creating of a symbolic burden bearer (or more than one). Using large packing boxes, students build the structure, then paint it with markers to resemble stones.

When this is completed the students move to tables containing actual stones of all shapes and sizes and a large laundry bag for each group (limit stones to manage weight). Working in groups of six or eight, students label all the stones with sins and suffering they carry around with them: Sins that need forgiving (for example, cruelty to others in thought, word, and deed). Sins of omission—all the things you meant to do but never got around to. Be specific. Label other stones for sinful thoughts. Also label sufferings, physical, mental, spiritual, e.g., birth is suffering/old age is suffering/sickness and death are suffering/to be separated from a loved one is suffering/to be vainly struggling to satisfy needs is suffering. We name the experience sufferable and the naming alone helps us bear it.

Place these burdens in the laundry bag and hoist them onto the back of one of the group members.

This student tries walking around the room with the burdens. At one point, the student backs up to the burden bearer to experience how resting for a moment relieves some of the pressure. If your structure is too flimsy, let it be just a symbolic burden bearer and use a stationary object such as a high table for the actual experience. Or two students can lock hands to create the burden-bearer structure.

Give all students who wish this experience of carrying the burdens.

Development of Theme

Talk with the group about the experience. Ask: Are you carrying burdens you don't need to carry? Does naming suffering and sins help? Can you leave your sins and sufferings at the foot of the burden bearer? Can you accept forgiveness and continue on your way lightened? Suffering is the breaking point of faith for many. It can crush the human spirit and jeopardize the possibility of belief.

Sing: "What a Friend We Have in Jesus" or a similar hymn from your tradition.

Following the singing, the groups open the laundry bags and take those stones which are labeled with forgivable sins and easable sufferings and place them in an altar-like arrangement at the base of the burden-bearer structure.

Group sings or listens to the hymn, "Be Still, My Soul" or another suitable hymn or song.

Leader: But sometimes in life there are burdens we cannot set down. We simply must bear them. A story of great pathos is told in our Scriptures. Samuel the prophet loved, chose, and anointed King Saul to rule over the people of Israel, but over the years the relationship between the two deteriorated, resulting finally in a deep split between them. In a final slash of division, they parted, and we read these haunting words of Scripture: "Samuel never again saw the king but he grieved over him."

Have you had experiences in your life, or known of experiences of alienation where the chasm is too wide to cross—the abyss between two persons too deep for reconciliation?

Is it possible, do you think, for a situation to develop that cannot be reconciled? The Bible seems to say so. To forgive would be to trivialize. It is not personal pride that keeps the person from forgiving. It is too deep. The love is still there, but the tie is broken. Forgiveness in this case may simply be the acceptance of the reality that has wounded. Some physical sufferings fall in this same category. The Lord said to Samuel: "How long will you go on grieving over Saul?"

Are there still stones in your bag? Burdens that you feel cannot be relieved, or suffering that must be borne? Jesus is our Burden bearer here also. Sometimes Jesus says, "I will take your burdens." Other times he says, "I will help you bear them."

As Christians we look to the suffering Jesus for help. In the midst of suffering, Jesus affirmed God's love. He affirmed life as being meaningful. He showed us that even in the midst of suffering, love is possible.

The mystery of human suffering remains. So long as evil exists, suffering will also exist. But Christ is our Burden bearer, going with us, bringing us to places of momentary rest. The burdened soul is restored, lifted up, filled with Christ's presence.

Closure

Prayer: We thank you, Lord, that you are our Burden bearer. We thank you that we can take our griefs and sufferings to you and at least for a little while rest them in your presence.

The Dew Man

Get the road ready for the Lord.
Make a straight path for him to
travel.

John 1:3

Symbols help us interpret reality. There is a beautiful symbol that comes to us from a third-world country. In the dense, equatorial, forests of Africa, a leader goes forth before the people and breaks the morning path for them. He takes upon himself the webs, the snares, and the accumulated dew. He is called the Dew Man. For Christians in some parts of Africa the Dew Man has become a symbol of Christ. Christ is our Dew Man as we seek to follow him.

In this service, a specific person is chosen as the Dew Man. He or she is dressed fantastically in streamers of ribbons and crepe paper, with bells at wrists and ankles and holding open tambourines with ribbon streamers. The face is made up with fantastic colors and symbols. This Dew Man leads members of the class to four pits that they must overcome if they are to be followers of the Dew Man and arrive at the clearing.

The pits are:

1. Quicksand of letting go
2. Bog of self-pity
3. Trap of self-concern
4. Snare of pride

A different room may be set up for each pit, or sections of your classroom may be used. At each pit, a scripture is read and an activity experienced.

Pit 1: Quicksand of Letting Go

Dew Man: Can you give yourself totally to following my way of belief? It is a perilous journey. First, you must really want to go. I will lead the way, but each of you must cross the pit by yourself. Your challenge here at the first pit is not to do anything new but simply to cease doing something. You have only to let yourself go. You must trust. The very nature of life and following the Dew Man is confidence. We can relax without controlling expectation. We will encounter quicksand here. Quicksand is loose, deep, wet sand in which a person can be swallowed up. If you fight or struggle, you sink. If you step lightly and gently, you cross.
Scripture: Luke 12:22-31

Activity: A Trust Circle.
The group forms a close circle, hands in front of each person, palms up. Someone stands in the center of the circle, eyes shut, feet together, arms crossed across chest. The center person falls back in trust. Gently the members of the circle catch and push the trusting person

around and across the circle. Give everyone in the group a chance to be in the center. When all have had this experience the Dew Man says:

> You have passed your first
> obstacle. You were able to stop
> operating, achieving, managing,
> controlling, planning and defending
> in order to simply be. Follow me
> to the Bog of Self-Pity.

Pit 2: Bog of Self Pity

Dew Man: Many of us were raised to think poorly of ourselves and have deeply rooted feelings of inferiority. Now we move beyond. Accept yourself. Accept your talent. Everyone has some handicap. Without total acceptance of ourselves, we will avoid what we most fear or hate in ourselves. How do we get through? A bog is spongy ground where we can become stuck. Self-pity can trap us in this bog. We must deal with this before we journey onward.

Scripture:

> People who are well do not need a
> doctor but only those who are sick.
> I have not come to call respectable
> people but outcasts.
>
> Mark 2:17

Experience: Divide the group into small groups of four each. Each member of the group draws a slip of paper with a description on it:

1. Blindfolded
2. Feet tied together
3. Arms tied together
4. Crawl on all fours

Following the instructions on the slips of paper, leaders help the team prepare itself. No. 1 is blindfolded; no. 4 gets on knees and hands; nos. 3 and 4 are tied.

When all are ready, the team is given a brief time-frame in which to cross to a designated spot at a distance where the Dew Man is waiting for them. All members of the team must make it to the destination and all must come together. The team works together to help all persons. If a team does not make it in the set time, they are given another opportunity. Continue at the activity until all have made it through the bog.

Dew Man receives those who overcame the pit: "Congratulations—you made it through Self-pity. You are a part of the universe. You have the right to be here. This is your time. You deserve to live it fully. You have a right to happiness and all good things. Accept yourself as made in the image of God."

We believe in our human potential. Our divine creative nature is celebrated. With this acceptance we can open the flood-gates of compassion.

(Group continues to Pit 3)

Pit 3: Trap of Self-concern

Dew Man: This is a dangerous obstacle, the fierce imprisonment in self. Self-concern seeks to fill all your thoughts. The trap of self-concern snaps shut tightly, and we are caught and imprisoned. How will you deal with selfishness? Natural life is self-centered. Something in us wants to be petted and admired, wants to take advantage of others, to exploit the whole universe. The jungle is very dense. If we do not follow our leader, we become half-crazed and lost and blinded. We wander off the path and are lost in deep undergrowth.

Here you faced the terrible alternative of choosing God or self for the center of your life. Whom will you follow?

Scripture: Luke 9:23

> If any one wants to come with me, he must
> forget himself, take up his cross everyday,
> and follow me.

Activity: A long line is drawn across the room with chalk or masking tape. Members of the teams, one at a time, must walk the line backwards looking only through a mirror they hold in front of them. They must not look down or around. You might wish to make the game more exciting by putting a time limit on walking the line or divide into teams and see which group finishes first.

Dew Man: You avoided this trap by looking outside yourself. You were able to make it through by focusing on something other than yourself. We can no longer assume that the world was created just for us. Now only one pit remains.

Pit 4: Snare of Pride

Dew Man: The essential vice, the most dangerous pit, is pride. A snare is a noose that jerks tight against the body and captures you. So is pride. Pride makes us feel right and righteous. Others are wrong. We rationalize our own way. We seek to control even the Dew Man, telling him where to go and how.

Scripture: Isaiah 2:11-12

> A day is coming when human pride will be
> ended and human arrogance destroyed.
> Then the Lord alone will be exalted. On that
> day the Lord Almighty will humble everyone
> who is powerful, everyone who is proud
> and conceited.

Activity: Push a Peanut

Using the same line as in Activity 3, each individual must get down on the floor and push a peanut with his or her nose from one end of the line to the other. Set a time limit in which this activity must be accomplished, or do this activity as a relay race between teams.

Dew Man: Pride causes us to assume we are all-powerful and have all the answers. This separates us from God. We humble ourselves. We have a transparent self-acknowledging of our weakness. With humor we see what ridiculous creatures we are, just as we looked and felt ridiculous pushing the peanut. Our crowded environment, jerky bodies, and driven feelings are a testimony to our weakness. But we affirm that our weakness reveals God's strength. We no longer take life for granted. It is a gift from God. There is a grace in all things.

Dew Man: You have tromped through the maze of temptations. I have gone before you to clear your path.

Now you have arrived at a clearing. The clearing is luminous, light and spacious, warm and full. It is open and simple. The clearing we seek is present right where we are, but it is hidden by our driving feelings, just as our way here was hidden by pits.

Now you can rest for a while here in the clearing. Resting teaches us that it is not so much what I do that makes me worthwhile as what I am for I am always more than I do in life or fail to do.

(Refreshments may be served here.)

Closing

Your life is like this journey. God is always calling us to new lands and into new adventures. Obstacles and pits will always be along the way. There is an ever present threat of evil and ways in which we are bound and trapped. But we avoid the pain of a life that has no great direction when we follow the Dew Man. Having a vision in life is crucial. This vision sustains us through the difficult choices and tests of life. Such a vision comes to us through the life/death/resurrection of Jesus.

We can experience Christ leading us through our own darkness, death, and guilt to a new understanding of forgiveness and life and resurrection. Listening to and accepting this Good News enables us to make it.

And through it all remember:

> There is nothing in all creation that will ever
> be able to separate us from the love of God
> which is ours through Christ Jesus our Lord.
> Romans 8:39

Holy Week

All Lent leads up to a special week. This is the one week in our church calendar that we call holy. This is the week we enter the great mystery, Jesus' death/resurrection, and we remember all that God has done through Jesus for us.

All church school members should be encouraged to participate as fully as possible in this week's celebration. Included here are three suggestions particularly appropriate to church school settings.

1. **A Palm Sunday-in-the-classroom drama** and creative activity for elementary and above.
2 **An intergenerational Maundy Thursday twilight supper.**
3. **An Easter morning celebration** in the classroom for children.

Palm Sunday: Different Voices

Palm Sunday is a familiar day of celebration in most churches. This very familiarity can cause some problems for us in the church school. When something becomes too familiar, it no longer speaks to us with power. How can we recapture the joy, complexity, and power of this occasion?

Palm Sunday is a day of great irony and contrast, the triumphant entry/the gathering storm. To approach this familiar story in a new way the class reads again our traditional stories: Luke 19: 28-40; John 12:12-19; Matthew 21:1-11; and Mark 11:1-10. These scriptures tell the story from four different points of view.

We always see things from our limited point of view. An adding together of several viewpoints deepens our understanding. We consider the story from still other angles. What would be the viewpoint not only of people, but of personified objects on that day?

In this program, four readers take the part of four objects: a palm branch, a thornbush, a spider, and a clay pot.

The use of limited points of view (suggested by the limited view of these objects) add odd voices to our story. They enable us to walk round and round the same event with several voices, from several places, iterating the same event. With the four scriptures as starters, encourage your class to add other viewpoints to this story. Palm Sunday took place outdoors—natural objects might speak. It took place with a large number of persons of all ages present. What objects might they have had? This personification of objects present on Palm Sunday is a device that helps us halt the flow of time and step back and look at an event with new eyes.

Outline

Step 1: Read the four scriptures.

Step 2: The four readers speak.

Step 3: Class members think of an object that might have been present on Palm Sunday. Personify the object and try to see the event from its limited point of view. Don't add any more than the object could see.

Step 4: Allow time for the creative development, then share the event as seen by the individual objects. Whole new dimensions to the story will emerge. No one can grasp it all, but individual voices speak and our picture becomes more complete.

The voices of objects, grotesque and imaginative, add a layer of irony to the story. Allow the imagination full range. Palm Sunday is not just about a triumphant parade but is a complex prelude to the Easter drama.

As we reflect on objects, we reflect upon creation, its wisdom and goodness. We reflect upon ourselves, more than flesh and blood and bone, and we consider Jesus, how he overcame death.

Voices

The Thorn-bush speaks: I have grown here beside this road for many years. I have seen many pilgrims trudge upward past me to the gates of the city of Jerusalem.

I am squatty, dust-covered. Most people avoid me because of my prickly spikes. I have reached out and grabbed donkey hair and sheep's wool when those stupid animals came too close. These ugly thorns protect me. I would be devoured without them. Camels and goats eat anything. They come sniffing and licking. My hardness and razor-sharp points discourage them.

The wild pattern of my branches break up the winds that would flatten me. Lacking beauty, I struggle to survive as best I can.

I am rewarded by shouts of pain when humans seek to catch hold of me. Some have learned from me and use my branches to torture and beat others. I bite into human skin easily and mercilessly. The thin skin covering is very easy for me to penetrate.

Today a parade went by. A man, with a different look somehow, went by on a donkey. Men, women, and children crowded around. Of course, they all avoided me and I got a good glimpse of it all. There was something in the face of that man that I have never glimpsed in another face.

Then a weasely looking man, dressed elegantly in silks and velvets, paused beside me. He stood there long after the parade had passed by.

He took a knife from his sash and slashed off one of my branches. Mumbling to himself he twisted my branch, limbering it, shaping it, fashioning it into a circle. He kept mumbling to himself: "You see, you see. We are not succeeding at all. Look, the whole world is following him."

The Palm Branch speaks: I have a lovely dwelling place. Here I stand on a small rise above the winding road leading to the gates of Jerusalem. The breezes ripple through my boughs making me sway and dance. The sunlight dapples my leaves. My fronds dip gracefully right over the roadway. Because of this, I have often been involved in these parades. It is a simple matter to reach up and break off one of my graceful branches. I don't mind. A couple of weeks ago a small group of persons was going up to Jerusalem to plead for pardon for some crime or other. They broke my branches and waved them low in front of them and moaned dismally.

I like it better when my branches are waved as signs of status and power. This happens sometimes. Mighty warriors have galloped by here. The people wave my branches and scream. Today's parade was different from any other I have ever seen. There was such a feeling of joy. It was mostly the children who picked my branches and waved them. Ah, those beautiful, dark-eyed, barefoot children. They were on top of the world, laughing, smiling at that man on the donkey. The people were calling him "King," but I don't know. He is like no king I have ever seen, or warrior either. A funny thing about him. There was such a glow from his face, a radiance really. My sun-speckled branches dimmed in comparison. He glowed with an inner light that somehow made all the rest look like it was in shadows. There is something different here. There is a deep sense of excellent graces that shine in him.

The Spider speaks: Few noticed me that day. I had built my web among the bushes by the roadside. There in my untidy scaffolding I lurked, waiting for victims to get trapped on my sticky threads. I am so small and well camouflaged that I can watch others, without being noticed myself. I noticed him ride by on that donkey that day. I sensed something in him that I longed to cry out about and warn him. "Watch out!" I wanted to cry. You see, I have many enemies, too. Birds and shrews are often after me, and larger spiders and hunting wasps, too. I have come to recognize that look and be on the defensive. But he wasn't. I saw his enemies here. Most people were shouting "Hosannah," but a few were only watching with that look in their eyes that said, "Just wait. I am after you."

"Build some means of defense," I wanted to cry. He looked so vulnerable. "Don't you know about pursuing prey? Don't you know how they creep up on a possible victim and then pounce and grab it? Don't you know how they lie in wait in their lairs until just the right moment, then move in for the kill? Don't you know? Don't you care?"

I know how camouflage and stillness allow them to trap unwary victims. I use this method myself. We create snares and wait until the prey becomes entangled. I see this happening to you. Don't you?

I know what it is like to be hated, to frighten others even when you aren't dangerous. Wake up, Man. Look around you. You are surrounded by enemies. Their fangs and jaws are ready to inject poison.

Why do you seem so unafraid?

The pot speaks: I am just a simple clay pot dug from the ground, kneaded and shaped by skillful hands. I have lain by the roadside since the day my owner dropped me here. On the day of the parade, there was such confusion. Sandals trampled me, working me into the ground. I remember a jumble of toes and heels and animal hoofs. At one point a cloak was thrown over me, then jerked up as the parade passed by. I barely glimpsed the man on the donkey. But he threw out something fresh and beautiful from the skin of his body. A fragrance. Once I had been carried by a field of blossoming trees in spring. It was the same fragrance.

Then a lovely woman stopped, loosened me where I was embedded in the soil. She looked at me, then looked at the disappearing figure on the donkey. She seemed to have some sort of vision of what I could be, a vision somehow shaped by the man on the donkey. "I'll plant flowers." I heard her say. "You, little clay pot, will be a container for something beautiful."

Maundy Thursday: A Family Supper

Maundy Thursday is another special day that does not take place on a Sunday. A different day, a different hour, and a different setting can help emphasize its importance. The following service is intergenerational, for all members of the church school five years old and above, and best held about 5:30 on Maundy Thursday evening. It can be publicized and promoted through church school channels.

Room arrangement is important. A fellowship hall or large gathering room is set up before time with twelve tables with seven chairs at each, placed in a circle around the room. One table (preferably round) is placed in the center. It is set with the communion elements. On each of the twelve surrounding tables there are palm fronds (from Palm Sunday). These leaves are the base for arrangements of fresh fruit (e.g., bananas, grapes, apples, pineapple, strawberries, nectarines).

A candle is on each table.

The tables are set for dinner service, and in addition to the fresh fruit which is to be eaten, include round loaves of bread, a sauce dish of honey butter, a plate of cheese wedges, wooden skewers, and a serrated knife. A beverage table is set up nearby.

A card with information about a disciple is on each table. A piano is helpful. The lights are dimmed and a worshipful atmosphere is created. The participants are held outside the room until the hour for beginning.

The group enters as one and takes seats at the twelve tables, sitting with families. A candle-lighter is ready.

You will, of course, want to adjust these arrangements to suit your audience. Tables can be combined for smaller groups. More than one service can be held if there are large numbers.

Opening: We welcome you to this service. Let us pause and recall the disciples.

As the candle is lit on each table will someone from that table stand and read the card remembering your disciple?

Table 1: *Phillip* is a Greek name, but I am of Jewish stock. My parents called me Phillip probably because of the famous governor whose son was Alexander the Great.

Table 2: I am *Matthew*, also called Levi. I was a customs officer, or tax collector.

Table 3: My name is *Thomas*. I am to be remembered by my doubting moments, rather than by my faith in Jesus.

Table 4: I, *Bartholomew*, remain largely unknown. Tradition has it that I carried the gospel to India.

Table 5: I am *Simon*. Not to be confused with Simon Peter. I was a Zealot, one of the major political parties of the Jews.

Table 6: *James* is my name. I am the "younger" disciple by that name, and brother of Matthew.

Table 7: I, *Judas*, am among the most famous disciples, but for the saddest of reasons.

Table 8: *James* is my name. My brother and I are known as sons of thunder.

Table 9: *Simon Peter* is my name. A fisherman by trade, I learned also to be a disciple.

Table 10: I am *Andrew*. Although more people know my brother, Peter, than know of me.

Table 11: I am *Thaddeus*. Not much is written of me, but my other name is Jude and the shortest book of the New Testament is mine.

Table 12: *John* is a common name. But I am grateful that history calls me the "beloved disciple."

Minister or leader reads the Scripture which is the first focus of the hour: Exodus 12:3-17, the record of Passover.

Then, let the instructions be given to all. One person only from each table is "runner" to get the beverages. No one else gets up, please. As the runners quietly serve others, the rest of the group practices the music to be used later if it is not familiar to them.

The meal of memory and fellowship is enjoyed. The persons at tables eat together the simple supper of bread and honey-butter, cheese, fruit and beverage.

Following the meal, the group reads responsively Psalm 118, part of the psalter that Judaism may have used in the Passover setting.

Minister (or Leader) then reads the New Testament account of the Last Supper found in Matthew 26:17-30.

In the midst of all the stir of the Passover festival, Jesus chose a meal with his disciples as the way he wanted to be remembered. What is it about eating together that means so much to all of us? How much of joy, of sorrow, of love, of memory is marked by eating together. It's true we often feel a stronger intimacy and companionship as we share a meal. Conversations seem to take on a personal quality like at no other time. We relax. We seem able to give our full attention to others when at table together. And Jesus chose just such an occasion to say. "Remember me—this way."

The Sacrament is served to each table. The bread is broken in each table setting from the loaves used in the just-completed supper. (Have a spare loaf on hand in the event some table(s) eat all theirs during the meal.) When all have a crust of bread the leader directs the singing of "Eat This Bread." Then the cup is passed by the minister (or the tray of cups, probably; if several trays are available they are given to alternate tables, and someone at each table can serve it to those seated there). When all have received the juice, they are invited to sing again, "Eat This Bread."

The leader may then read the closing verses of the New Testament passage, indicating that when the disciples had received the supper they sang a hymn and withdrew to the Mount. "What Wondrous Love Is This" or "Tis Midnight and on Olive's Brow" may be appropriate ones to use, either of them, prior to the dismissal. As the hymn is ended, the leader bids them goodnight until we meet again for the Good Friday vigil (or the Easter Sunrise Service).

In quietness, the families leave in expectation of gathering again to recall and re-enact further events of Jesus' life.

Easter Day: Life Is Beautiful!

Resurrection cannot be explained to children. It is a mystery. But a burst of praise and resurrection joy can be experienced. The place impacts on the event, and we seek to create an environment in our classroom of radiant, efficacious color. This service is for Easter Sunday morning in the church school classroom setting. Recommended for first and second grade.

Before time: On a previous Sunday or weekday, children have created a tomb cave by taking brown paper grocery bags and streaking them with colored chalk. Then the paper is crushed to form a rock. The "rocks" are fastened to a large cardboard box turned on its side to form a cave.

Room setup for Easter morning: The tomb cave is placed in one corner of the room. On one wall is a long graffiti sheet with crayons nearby. Two tables are set up for craft work. One contains food coloring in muffin tins and rolls of paper towels for Easter banners. The other one contains construction paper and Easter stickers and decals, and butterfly stickers for hands.

The teacher greets the children as they gather: Today is our very special day in the church. This is the Sunday of Sundays. This is the day we are overwhelmed by God's victory and the vastness of divine love and mercy. This is a day like rainbows filling the world. This is a day of bright and beautiful colors, the most beautiful we can imagine.

After children have gathered, the teacher reads the Easter story from Luke 24:1-12.
The class then acts out the story.

Teacher says: "Our happy, happy day starts sadly. We are all disciples going to the tomb. We will walk sadly, slowly. At first it is a very sad time."

Class approaches the tomb. (If the cave has not been prepared ahead of time, drape a sheet or blanket over two portable chalk boards or suspend it from the ceiling to create an empty tomb.)

Teacher: The angel at the tomb said: "Jesus is not here. He is risen, but he left you many colors." (Colored crepe paper, in either long strips or gently twirled and made into necklaces, are draped over all the students' heads.)

Teacher:

Here is yellow for happiness and prosperity.
Here is green for growth and newness.
Here is red for excitement and aliveness.
Here is blue for faith and virtue.
Here is white for protection from heaven.
Here is purple, the color of kings
Here is gold, precious and shining.

(Pile many garlands over each student until they all look like rainbows.)

Teacher: Jesus wants you to spread the Good News through bright colors.

This is a day of opposites. You, the disciples, thought you were going to be sad, but you are made very happy. Life has lots of opposites. Let's listen.

Opposites

If things always went *up*
  like balloons from a string,
But never came *down*
  like a ball to the ground,
What a strange world it would be.

If the sun always shone
  and we never had rain,
If we always were happy
  and never had pain,
What a strange world it would be.

If things always were *loud*
  like sirens and screams,
And never were *quiet*
  like furry shoes seem,
What a strange world it would be.

If you always tasted *sharp* things
    like icycles' tips,
And never drank *smooth* things
    like cool water sips,
What a strange world it would be.

 If you could only smell roses
    gentle and light,
And never spicy chili
    on a cold, winter night,
What a strange world it would be.

But God had a plan for life to be full
Of all different things—a back and forth pull.

An up and down swing,
An in and out prance,
A high and low fling,
A round and round dance.

Listen—oh listen
To God's secret we hark,
There always comes daylight
After the dark.

Once we were sad
For Jesus was dead.
Today he lives;
We are singing instead.
What a wonderful world it can be.

Teacher: This poem reminds us that there are a lot of opposite things in the world. We have all known sad days. It was a sad day when Jesus died. But today is a happy day, the happiest day of all for us because Jesus is alive. We want to think about and remember other happy days in our lives. On the graffiti sheet write or draw the happiest day in your life. (Students work on graffiti sheet, covering the paper with colors and happy events.) When this is completed, students look at each other's work.

Ask students: What can you learn about happiness by looking at these pictures? What can we learn about our friends?

Then, gathered around their mural, they sing "All Things Bright and Beautiful."

Craft Table 1
Teacher: Let us continue to spread color through the world. (Children are instructed to go to craft tables. At one table they create paper fans. First they decorate a sheet of colored

construction paper with Easter stickers and decals. Then they fold the paper, accordian-style, into a fan.)

Teacher explains how the fans are a beautiful Easter symbol. Jesus was dead and buried (the fan is closed); on Easter Day he arose (fan is opened)!

Craft table 2
Children make dip-and-dye paper banners.

Step 1:   Vegetable food coloring is put in muffin tins and a small amount of water is added.

Step 2:   Children fold a square of paper toweling (heavy, quilted kind). Experiment with different folds, triangle, tight folds, etc.

Step 3:   Child dips a corner of the towel into the food coloring. Let the color seep in but do not saturate the paper.

Step 4:   Child turns the paper and dips another section in the same color or a different one.

Step 5:   Unfold *carefully*.

Step 6:   Dry.

Step 7:   Surround the room with paper banners. Tape some together to form a large banner.

Closure

As the students leave, the teacher places a butterfly sticker in both palms of each child. She says, "Close your fists; Jesus is dead and buried. Open your palms and show your butterfly. He is risen!"

Pentecost: Noises

On the day of Pentecost, we celebrate the coming of the Holy Spirit and the beginning of the Christian church. A foundational theme of Pentecost is that the gospel is proclaimed in every tongue and in every place unto all the world.

Following is an adaptation of the Pentecost story that children can experience in the classroom. A teacher and simple rhythm instruments (gourd rattles, tambourines, and bongo drums) are needed.

Before the Story:
   1. Practice "gibberish" with the class. In gibberish, students speak with the inflection, tone, and rhythm of ordinary speech, but they use nonsense words or syllables. Have the students practice by turning to their neighbor and speaking in an unknown tongue. Instruct them to all speak simultaneously in gibberish when you give them the signal during the story.

2.   Hand out the instruments to individual children. Instruct them to hold the instruments silently until you motion for them to play.

Pentecost Story

Teacher: Pentecost began in silence. Many, many people were gathered together, but they were silent. There was the silence of fear. These people were afraid for their very lives. Their leader Jesus had been killed, and authorities were still on the lookout for signs of rebellion. In fear the people hid together in an upper room. Thick walls muted the sound of their whispering voices.

There was the silence of despair. Hearts were uplifted and thrilled when word spread that Jesus had risen, but that was fifty days ago—fifty long, despairing days. Now the people sat silent, some trying to pray, some simply staring into space.

Then a rustling sound began. (Rattle one gourd.)

The sound grew louder. (Add six more rattles or as many as you have, one at a time.)

And louder still. (Add as many tambourines as you have, one at a time.)

The people jumped up and looked around. The whole silent house was vibrating with the sound. What is this strange noise? Where was it coming from? It sounded a little like a wind, but outside the window no trees bent in the breeze, no debris swirled. Only in this house, in this place, did the strange sound occur. (Continue rattling gourds and shaking tambourines.)

Then, just as mysteriously as it had come, the sound went away. (Silence.)

Now, before their startled eyes, a strange sight began to appear. It pulsed like a tongue of fire. (Drum or bongo drum beats pattern: heavy, light, light, light, heavy, light, light, light.)

The tongues reached out and touched each person present. (Continue drums.)

The people felt themselves warmed in a mysterious way. They looked around and saw others glowing in the same mysterious manner. (Drum beat continues.)

Now the room was alive with sounds—all sorts of strange languages and words, like gibberish. (Children speak in nonsense syllables, gibbering.)

And yet—and yet these garbled words make sense and others could hear and understand.

Listen to the room now. (Include rattles, tambourines, drums, and gibberish.) (Stop sounds.)

Then all the followers of Jesus, the disciples and all who were gathered there, knew that something wonderful had happened. The Holy Spirit that Jesus had promised to send had come.

The people burst from the room to share the news with every one in town. The silence of fear was gone. The silence of despair had vanished. The promised presence of God had come with power and might.

Group sings, "I'm Gonna Sing When the Spirit Says Sing!" Accompany with rhythm instruments.

Another Classroom Idea for Pentecost

Get thirty pictures, taken from magazines and related to the Pentecost theme (winds, fires, the color red, etc.). Use the pictures to start conversation.

THE LESSER FESTIVALS

We need the Church Year in our lives because prosperity has thrown many of us off balance. The rhythm of the Church Year stabilizes us. I remember my mother saying that as a child, she only had oranges at Christmas, and what a wonderful, jubilant occasion it was when the Christmas boxes of oranges arrived. In my own lifetime, I remember when we only ate turkey at Thanksgiving, and it was a mouth-watering, eye-delighting spectacular. But now our grocery stores are piled high with pyramids of oranges, and every other week we eat low cholesterol turkey. What was once festive has become routine, and the edge has been taken off the festivals. We are jaded with too many good things. The saying "Too much of a good thing" rings true in many of our lives.

I live in a community that is popular for weddings. Since I am married to a minister, I am involved in many of these occasions. I tell myself these are very special times in the lives of the participants, but week after week after week of weddings dulls the sense of celebration. There can be even too much of flowers and music and food and party clothes. We can even grow weary of these beautiful things.

The Church Year, faithfully followed, restores the balance of our lives. We celebrate the stark beauty of Lent. We fast with only liquids so that our party-saturated bodies are restored and our spirit, wobbly with too many good things, gets on an even keel again.

Our celebrations are tied more closely to God and God's purpose for our lives. Madison Avenue does not tell us how to celebrate. We do not keep doing just one more thing every year until at Christmas our rooms are clogged with presents. And at Mother's Day. And Grandparents Day. And Secretary's Week. And birthdays, and Valentine's, and Superbowl Sunday, and Mardi Gras, until we whirl around in an orgy of holidays and never stop to ask what it is we celebrate.

We look at Jesus' life: We see his moments of high hilarity balanced with solitary searching.

We have tended in churches of the Free traditions to ignore Holy Innocents Day, Ascension Day, Transfiguration Day, and All Saints Day with their more somber themes, especially in the church school and especially with children. But as we look to the Church Year for balance, these special days invite us to consider, to ponder, to recognize that the hurting moments of our lives, the frightened moments, the desperate moments, are also what it means to be human and under the protective wing of God. This section of the book contains services for these days in the Church Year. These are services to be observed or prepared for in the classroom setting.

Holy Innocents Day
(Children of War)

There are some lesser holidays observed in more liturgical churches that can speak to us with power if we remember the formula of looking first with fresh eyes at the basic human condition, situation, or need to which the holiday speaks. One such holiday, observed in Catholic, Lutheran, and Episcopal churches is Holy Innocents Day.

This festival occurs on December 28. At first it seems a horrible paradox that in the midst of our Christmas celebrations glorifying children and joy and laughter, we read the story of the children murdered by Herod in his attempt to destroy Jesus. Yet the story has a gripping contemporary message as we are made aware through television and news media of the innocent children killed daily in our present wars.

Though Holy Innocents Day is seldom celebrated in free tradition Protestant churches, we often have a program on peace. These two themes can be combined. Children in the church school and parents can hear the message of peace in a new way through the scriptures and theme of Holy Innocents Day.

This biblical story found in Matthew 2:16-18 is part of our Christian heritage and can be inculcated into our religious training. The feeling-level of this story is horror and revulsion. It is injustice and rage. Innocent and defenseless children are martyred! Yet our Christian faith speaks a word of hope even in this situation.

The following program is suggested as a way to observe Holy Innocents Day. The setting is a church school classroom where special work has gone into the creating of a specific environment (see instructions below). The program is powerful if presented by elementary children for adults of the congregation, but may also be presented by youth or adults. The theme is "Remember Our Children."

Room Environment:
If possible obtain the names of children killed in wars, any war throughout history. This may prove difficult because children have always been the nameless victims. But using an actual name can be very powerful and bring an immediacy and contemporary aspect to the event. One way to obtain names may be to ask soldiers or former soldiers in your community if they know the names of any child victims. Perhaps

someone in your church has had a child relative killed as the result of a war. If you discover one or two names it may be enough. The name Samantha Smith (the little girl who wrote and visited Russia), though not a victim of war, is a symbol of peace. Anne Frank, who was killed in World War II; the four black children killed in Birmingham in 1963; Sadako, killed as a result of the atomic bomb, are others.

Designate a wall in your classroom as your Memorial Wall. Cover it with dark paper, then let children write, in their bold open handwriting, the names of the victims. Using a computer, print a large strip in black and white with the single word "Remember." Place this on your wall. Another possibility is to use pictures of children's faces from around the world. Remove or cover other decorations in your classroom. Arrange chairs for the audience facing the wall.

The Service

Tape recorded sound of weeping or appropriate music. After a time, the Old Testament reader stands and reads Jeremiah 31:15.

The Lord says

> A sound is heard in Ramah
> the sound of bitter weeping
> Rachel is crying for her children
> they are gone
> and she refuses to be comforted.

Sound effects used again, then:
New Testament reading: Matthew 2:13-18.

When Herod realized that the visitors from the East had tricked him, he was furious. He gave orders to kill all the boys in Bethlehem and its neighborhood who were two years old and younger. This was done in accordance with what he had learned from the visitors about the time when the star had appeared. In this way, what the prophet Jeremiah had said came true.

> A sound is heard in Ramah
> the sound of bitter weeping
> Rachel is crying for her children
> she refuses to be comforted.

Tape sound.

Leader: This story is part of our biblical tradition. For centuries this story has cried out to us from Scripture. How many children died that day? The population of Bethlehem has been estimated at perhaps three hundred. It is unlikely that there were more than twenty of these children. Yet each was precious in the eyes of God, and our toll of children has grown through the years. As we listen to these voices of children will you say after each reader:

"Pray for us."

Reader 1: Throughout history children have been the innocent victims of war. This is true even today. In Iran, Ireland, Lebanon, and South Africa, children are often placed at the head of demonstrations, marches, and funeral processions. We see it on television.

Audience response: Pray for us.

Reader 2: Children, with their more fragile body frames, are the first to suffer from the ravages that accompany war. War cripples children, hits them with bombs, kills them with diseases, leaves them to starve. Too young to choose, they die against their will.

Response: Pray for us.

Reader 3: In Africa, a mother tells that when the invaders came to her village, she only had time to take the hand of her child nearest to her and flee. The rest of her children were left behind.

Response: Pray for us.

Reader 4: Elizabeth Crawford lives in Ireland. "There were ten of us, seven brothers, two sisters, and myself. I was seven. My mother was killed in a crossfire between the IRA and the army. My brother was shot by mistake. Someone thought he was a policeman. My grandfather was run down by a car. We couldn't understand it. We didn't know where to turn or who to blame. We asked the adults, and they all had different views on it." Roger Rosenblatt, *Children of War*; Doubleday Anchor Books, 1984, pp. 48-49.)

Response: Pray for us.

Reader 1: Paul Rowe was seven when he saw his father shot to death. He says, "It doesn't matter who done it. Nothin's worth killing someone" (ibid., p. 35).

Response: Pray for us.

Reader 2: Kim Seng of Cambodia saw both of her parents die as the result of war. She says, "To me revenge means I must make the most of my life" (ibid., p.135).

Response: Pray for us.

(Add here the stories that accompany the specific names you have identified and that are on your Memorial Wall.)

All sing: "Jesus Loves Me"

Leader: We read a story in our Old Testament Scriptures about King David, engaged in a mighty battle. He expressed longing for a drink from the best well in his hometown of Bethlehem. Three of his men slipped through the enemy lines to fulfill his casual wish. David was overwhelmed when his men returned with this gift for which they had risked their lives. In a moment of deep appreciation, he poured the water on the ground as a libation to God because he could not drink what the men had brought at such great risk.

Symbolically, we pour this water (pour water from ewer into a basin) remembering peace has been bought at the great price of children's lives.

Leader: What word of hope is there for us?

"I hear a loud voice speaking from the throne: Now God's home is with mankind.

He will live with them and they shall be his people. God himself will be there and he will be their God. He will wipe away all tears from their eyes. There will be no more death, no more grief or crying or pain. The old things have disappeared" (Revelation 21:3-5).

After each of the following readings, will you please say, "Thanks be to God!"

Reader 1: God promises return and reward, a hopeful future, and a homecoming. Reports say that children play among the rubbles of war. That children's laughter is heard in desolate places.

Response: Thanks be to God.

Reader 2: What is peace? What does it mean? What happens in the world of children when there is war? Though it is not true of all, many children, victims of war, carry no hate in their hearts; they show a will to survive, and they are exceptionally gentle with grownups and each other.

Response: Thanks be to God.

Reader 3: Worries and doom predictions can be self-fulfilling. So can expectations about war. Let a little child lead us. Peacemaking is as heroic as making war. Peace can be just as much a cause for which to live as war.

Response: Thanks be to God.

Reader 4: "He will settle disputes among great nations. They will hammer their swords into plows and their spears into pruning knives. Nation will never go again to war. Never prepare for battle again. Now, descendants of Jacob, let us walk in the light which the Lord gives us" (Isaiah 2:4-5, TEV.)

Response: Thanks be to God.

Reader 5: The day of remembering the Holy Innocents is about evil and the working of evil. But life is good and a better world can come if this generation brings it about.

Response: Thanks be to God.

Leader: We can promise to remember.

(Pass out paper chain bracelets with a name of a child for each person present. White is an appropriate color. When all have received bracelets **Leader** says):

We can bless and hold our children out to the love of God. Stretch your arm with the bracelet on it in front of you, palm up. Hold out to the love of God those who have been hurt and all innocent children who might be hurt. Now hold out your other arm in the same way symbolizing those who have done the hurting, the Herods, the warmongers. Bless them too, so that they may turn their anger and violence and resentment to the light of love for healing. This blessing is hard. We are too hurt and too angry to have the least desire to bless. Yet we accept the brokenness and sin and violence in all of us and turn to God for transforming.

Closing Hymn: "Let There Be Peace on Earth."

Let There Be Peace on Earth

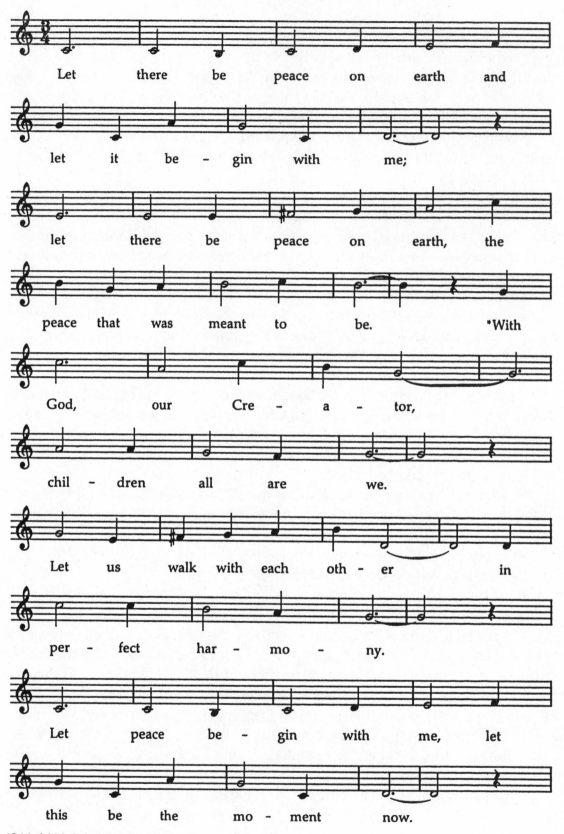

Let there be peace on earth and

let it be - gin with me;

let there be peace on earth, the

peace that was meant to be. *With

God, our Cre - a - tor,

chil - dren all are we.

Let us walk with each oth - er in

per - fect har - mo - ny.

Let peace be - gin with me, let

this be the mo - ment now.

*Original: With God as our Father, brothers all are we.

WORDS: Sy Miller and Jill Jackson
MUSIC: WORLD PEACE, Sy Miller and Jill Jackson

Let There Be Peace on Earth (cont'd)

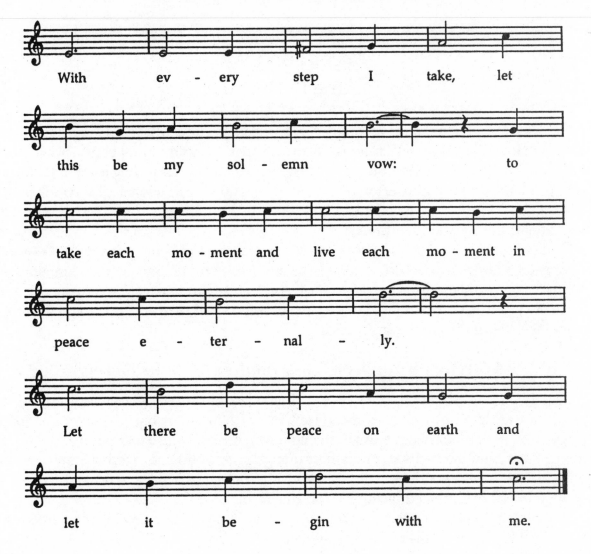

With ev - ery step I take, let this be my sol - emn vow: to take each mo - ment and live each mo - ment in peace e - ter - nal - ly. Let there be peace on earth and let it be - gin with me.

See also:

A charge to keep I have
Hail the day. . .
Jesus, Lord, we look to thee
O day of God, draw nigh
O holy city seen of John
O Spirit of the living God
We've a story to tell to the nations
When the church of Jesus

Ascension Day:
Time Between

One of the advantages we of the freer Protestant traditions have in using the Church Year is that we can take a celebration new to us, bare it to its structural bones, bring them to the surface and look with fresh eyes at them. We can touch the feeling level. Looking at Ascension Day had this impact for me. The story was familiar, but what is the core feeling? Where does our human experience intersect with this biblical story? Though not the traditional interpretation in liturgical churches, I was struck when contemplating this day, with the terrible feeling of abandonment, of being alone and being powerless. Between Ascension and Pentecost there was no Jesus and there was no Spirit, or so it must have seemed to the early disciples. It seems that every deep felt human feeling corresponds to a Bible story. We have experienced this feeling of being totally lost and alone, and the Bible story takes this feeling and transforms it.

A Service for Youth or Young Adults on Ascension Day

Step 1: As the youth enter, they are invited to think of someone who is leaving or whom you are leaving or who has already left, so that the relationship is being pulled apart physically. A death or divorce situation might be the separating experience.

After a few moments to collect these thoughts, the youth are asked to draw pictures of themselves saying goodbye in this situation on a large sheet of paper stretched across the wall. A mural of combined pictures will be the result.

Step 2: Following this the youth are seated in a semi-circle facing the mural. On a small table a large candle burns. Invite silence.

After a time, the leader reads Acts 1:3-23. For forty days after his death, he (Jesus) appeared to them many times in ways that proved beyond doubt that he was alive. He talked with them about the Kingdom of God, and when they came together, he gave them this order: Do not leave Jerusalem, but wait for the gift I told you about, the gift the Father promised. John baptized with water, but in a few days you will be baptized with the Holy Spirit.

When the apostles met together with Jesus, they asked him, "Lord, will you at this time give the Kingdom back to Israel?" Jesus said to them, "The times and occasions are set by my Father's own authority, and it is not for you to know when they will be. But when the Holy Spirit comes upon you, you will be filled with power and you will be witnesses for me in Jerusalem, in all of Judea and Samaria and to the ends of the earth.

After saying this, he was taken up to heaven as they watched him and a cloud hid him from their sight. They still had their eyes fixed on the sky as he went away when two men dressed in white suddenly stood beside them and said, "Galileans, why are you standing there looking up at the sky? This Jesus who was taken from you into heaven will come back in the same way that you saw him go to heaven."

Step 3: (Leader blows out the candle.)

Again, invite silence. Ask the class to think about the cold, hard core of loneliness. Then continue reading slowly:

"Then the disciples went back to Jerusalem from the Mount of Olives which is about a half a mile away from the city. They entered the city and went up to the room where they were staying."

Step 4: To help us get in touch with the feeling the disciples must have been experiencing, all of you will be blindfolded at the same time and asked just to experience this and act in any way that seems natural to you for three minutes. The only rule is: No attempt must be made to remove the blindfolds or try to peek through blindfolds.

(Blindfolds are placed on each person. Persons react in any way they like as the leader times this for three minutes. At the end of this time, blindfolds are removed and the youth return to the circle.)

Step 5: Discuss with the group what happened during this blindfolded period. What did you do? Walk around feeling things? Sit down and wait? Seek a way out?

What were your feelings?

Step 6: Leader: This feeling of being lost, of being deserted, of being utterly alone is a feeling we all experience at some time or other in our lives. Some of our best literature picks up this theme—the hero or heroine having to take an unmarked path—to go blindfolded as it were, into the future. The hobbit Frodo, in *The Lord of the Rings* trilogy, struggles at one point across the oppressive pits of Mordor. "No taste of food, no feel of water, no sound of wind, no memory of trees or grass or flower, no image of moon or stars are left to me. I am naked in the dark and there is no veil between me and the wheel of fire."

These words pick up the feeling level the disciples must have been experiencing as they faced the future without Jesus. Totally lost, terribly afraid, but they go on—back to the room where they are staying. I will follow Jesus though I do not know the way. Powerless and alone, they take the cup of courage. Can we imagine their despair? Their emotions must have ricochetted dramatically during those days. Jesus glorified on Palm Sunday, tried and crucified the next week, raised in glory following entombment, present with them again and now gone. They had a promise of a gift that was coming to sustain them. But not yet. Now they were between the times and it was dark and frightening.

We know that feeling in our lives; a separation, a parting can throw us completely off balance. Where can we turn? Where do we go when we are totally lost?

Our lives become tedious, being spent in an impatient expectation.

We are fortunate we know what happened next to the disciples. On Pentecost the Holy Spirit did come to be with them and give them power, but that is another story. What about us? When we are that lost and alone person, what do we do?

Step 7: Experience with me now a Shout of Despair.

Using words from Psalm 126, divide the group into two parts. One side, despair; one side, hope.

The "despair" group says in unison:

"Those who sow in tears"

The "hope" group in unison responds:

"Will reap with songs of joy."

The phrases are repeated alternately five times, each time getting louder until on the fifth time, the groups are shouting their words.

Now reverse sides. Giving the new despair side the words of Psalm 30:5:

"Weeping may [last] for a night"

and the new hope side the words:

"But joy will come with the morning."

(RSV)

Follow the same pattern of repeating alternately until the fifth time results in a loud shouting.

Step 8: Our scriptural message (Psalm 30:5) is, "Hold on—continue on the hard, unknowing path. Joy will come with the morning."

When Jesus was with the disciples he talked, healed, and loved them, and they felt the direct presence of God. To be in the company of Jesus was to be in the company of God. Now he was gone. We all experience times of separation from God. One Christian searcher, St. John of the Cross, called it "the dark night of the soul." Our Christian promise is: We can make it. Keep on keeping on. We feel panicky. We feel utterly lost, but we can outlast this panic. We can keep going. We are spooked and bedeviled, but there is light at the end of the tunnel. This separation is a very temporary condition. It is a human feeling experienced at some time or other in all our lives, but it only lasts a little while.

(Invite silence)

We know now, we who live after the giving of the Holy Spirit, that God has never really deserted us. Whatever it is, God is in it with us, working to heal that which is broken. God is with us in all our pain and grief and confusion—sharing, being, redeeming.

Our Christian promise is not only that we can bear the dark night but that dawn will come. But that's another story. Tonight as we recall the Ascension story, we remember the times between.

Step 9: Sing "Lonesome Valley."

Jesus walked this lonesome valley,
He had to walk it by himself.
Oh, nobody else could walk it for him
He had to walk it for himself.

We must walk this lonesome valley,
We have to walk it by ourselves.
Oh, nobody else can walk it for us,
We have to walk it by ourselves.

Disciple's Day:
A Sunflower Celebration

One of the most puzzling things about special days in the liturgical churches to us in the Free Church tradition is the many celebrations of individual saints' days. Some of the saints' days are for familiar biblical persons such as Peter or Paul. Other days commemorate persons who have lived but about whom we know little, such as Matthias and Barnabus. Still others seem to be mostly legendary, as St. George or St. Michael.

There are patron saints of parishes and missions, even whole countries, as St. George is considered the patron saint of England or St. Patrick of Ireland.

Before the Reformation, the clutter of saints' days had proliferated beyond control with every day of the year having several saints associated with it. The Reformers kept only the days of the twelve apostles and the four evangelists, but slowly certain other popular days crept in.

The saints' days included in many Lutheran, Anglican, and Roman Catholic calendars still seem formidable to us. A partial list follows:

St. Andrew	St. Thomas	St. Stephen
St. Paul	St. Peter	St. Matthias
St. Joseph	St. Mark	St. Phillip
St. James	St. Barnabas	St. John the Baptist
St. Mary	St. Bartholomew	St. Matthew
St. Michael	St. Luke	St. James of Jerusalem
St. Simon	St. Jude	St. Patrick

What can we glean from all this?

Certainly a celebration of the struggles of previous Christians can put us in touch with our roots and our sense of calling as Christian people. The witness of these people point to our potential as Christian witnesses. A careful study can reveal and identify certain masked urgings which have driven them to fashion exceptional lives, and we can look for those same urgings in our lives.

We do not have "saints" in our Free Church tradition, but we are aware of those persons who have led exceptional Christian lives. We think of Mother Teresa in our own time. And we acknowledge that children and adults need heroes. Perhaps we of the freer Protestant persuasion can take a cue here from our liturgical brethren. We have studied the lives of exceptional Christians but have not celebrated them.

Let me suggest an occasion here that can be celebrated in our church school classroom that picks up all heroes rather than a celebration of any one person. It gives students a chance to participate festively in recognizing those persons who have led exceptional God-pointed lives. It may be held during the regular church school hour or as an after-school activity.

Since the word "witness" is a more acceptable one to the freer Protestant tradition than "saint;" this celebration is called "Sunflower Witnesses." It is a joyous, exuberant, noisy celebration of exceptional Christians. This word "witness" also allows us more freedom in choosing women than does the word "heroes."

Sunflower Celebration

Before the celebration, each student decides on a particular witness. They are to choose someone who has lead an exceptional Christian life in our own time or in the past. It may be someone from your own church or community. If possible bring a picture of your witness. They may be from any walk of life as long as they have been a witness to others of God. Send a postcard to the students during the week to remind them to bring their witness' picture. The searching and deciding is an important part of the whole experience. In case anyone forgets, you might have on hand names and pictures such as: Bishop Desmond Tutu, Mother Teresa, Martin Luther King, Jr., John Wesley, Thomas Merton, Dorothy Day.

Step 1: As students arrive, they sit in a circle. Each tells the name of his or her witness, shows the picture, and tells a little about the life.

Step 2: When all have shared, the teacher says:

A sunflower is unique among all the other flowers. Some might describe its looks as rather ordinary. It grows alongside doors and fences and in simple gardens. But the unique thing about it is this: Every morning the sunflower's face turns up and follows the course of the sun all the day, drooping down at night as the sun sets. Day after day, this is the way it grows, getting taller, stronger, more resilient to the wind. Sometimes it grows seven feet tall by daily raising its seedheavy head and quenching a deep sun thirst. Even on days when the sun does not shine the sunflower waits, turned toward dawn. Each day it begins again, face lifted, turning, sun-yearning.

The witnesses that you have chosen are like sunflowers. They were not born as different from you and me, but at some point in their lives, they discovered or experienced God just as the sunflower discovers the sun. These persons know that God is the source of light and life. They simply turn their faces to God each day and try to follow God's light, growing stronger each passing hour. On difficult days they wait, knowing that God will come again, just as the sunflowers wait during cloudy times. These special persons have discovered something we also can discover. Having found God—the source of light—all other light, however strong, is not enough.

Step 3: Students adjourn to tables. Each is given a yardstick and a large sunflower cut from construction paper or tag board. They attach the picture of their witness to the center of the flower. If there is no picture, they write in the name. Then the sunflower is attached to the top of the yardstick.

Step 4: When all are ready the class parades around the room, perhaps even down the hall, holding high their sunflower witness and singing a good marching song such as, "We're Marching to Zion."

Step 5: Back in the classroom, the students tape the yardstick witnesses around the wall of the classroom. The students are surrounded with a cloud of witnesses. Then the students again assemble in a circle. The teacher explains:

"All of these sunflower witnesses have or had a dream for making the world a better place. Martin Luther King, Jr., in his speech during the March on Washington, August 28, 1963, spoke of his dream:

I have a dream that one day—the sons of former slaves and the sons of former slave owners will be able to sit down together at the table of brotherhood—I have a dream that my four little children will one day live in a nation where they will not be judged by the color of their skin but by the content of their character."

Take a few minutes to think in silence; then share:

(1.) What do you think your sunflower witness' dream for a better world is?

(2.) What deep wish do you have for making the world a better place for everyone to live?

Step 6: Share and discuss responses.

Step 7: If you have extra time, explain: One way to honor special persons is to mint a commemorative coin in their honor. (If you have a commemorative coin you might show it here.) We will make a commemorative coin honoring our witness.

Instructions:

Have aluminum pie tins for each student. Using a popsicle stick, push in a design from the back, remembering to reverse all the lettering!

All Saints Day
A Church Hour Presentation

All Saints Day originated in the early church as Christians sought a way to honor the many named and nameless saints and martyrs of the faith. In non-liturgical churches we do not canonize persons as "saints." This day becomes for us a way to celebrate the lives of ordinary Christians and of our love for those who are no longer with us. As people who belong to God, we are joined—past, present, and future. A member of our church (a saint) who has lived among us and worked alongside us is remembered after death. We feel a need to remember continually in order to soften the parting.

Traditionally, this is a one day celebration (November 1 or the Sunday nearest) that causes us to pause in the long season of Sundays after Pentecost.

This celebration can speak to us with meaning because, as Christians, we are the Saints of God, persons who belong to God. Often it is difficult to see the saint in others or recognize the saint within ourselves. Also, one who has lost a close one needs more than a one-time funeral. We need to continue to remember and grieve and express this.

The following suggested program is for the entire church congregation with empha-

85

sis on families and close friends of those members of the church who have died during the year. Though the service takes place during worship, preparation is made during church school.

Before the service, the children of the church school make banners including name and symbols that signify something from the life of a church member who has died during the year. For example, if the person were a church school teacher, an education symbol could be incorporated. There could be some reminder of their vocation, such as a carpenter's tool or a doctor's stethoscope. Eyeglasses or a Bible or a baseball bat could be used where appropriate. Words could be used as well, indicating some characteristic of the person like "wise" or "friendly." These could be cut from material and sewn on the banner. Someone who knew the person well could help with these symbols and words. A person from the congregation with artistic abilities could help with the designs.

If the deceased saint is a man, try to obtain a tie or several ties that he wore. Cut these into patterns and cover your banner. This has a dramatic and personal impact as well as providing texture for a rich mosaic.

If the deceased saint is a woman, try to obtain scarfs that she wore, or find out the colors she often wore and get squares of silk in these colors to cut into patterns and cover your banner. On All Saints Day the children process into the Sanctuary to the stirring hymn "For All the Saints Who from Their Labors Rest," sung by the entire congregation. The children carry the banners. They march down the aisle and around the congregation arriving at the front of the church.

An idea from the National Children's Conference of the United Methodist Church 1985, might be added here. In the narthex of the church, the entering church members would be invited to attach a small bell to ribbon streamers in all colors. Each bell represents a saintly person you remember in your life. These ribbon streamers would sway from crossed poles carried by the children. The ribbon standards with the softly jingling bells would be interspersed between the memorial banners in the opening procession.

Following the procession, the banners are placed on stands in a prominent place at the front of the church. The names are read aloud and the symbols explained.

The reading of each banner is followed by these words said together by the congregation:

"This is the way ___ understood life and its meaning." This is followed by a period of silent thanksgiving prayer for the contribution of that person's life.

Then the following liturgy unfolds.

Minister: We recall with love those who have died in the faith. Hear these words:

Reader 1: It was in faith that all these persons died. They did not receive the things God had promised but from a long way off they saw them and welcomed them and admitted openly that they were foreigners and refugees on earth (Hebrews 11:13).

Hymn

Reader 2: Saints are not long ago and far away heroes of the faith; saints are contemporary people who try to live bravely and faithfully, to love God and one another. We aspire to be saints, in honor preferring one another.

"After this I looked, and behold, a great multitude which no man could number, from every nation, from all tribes and peoples and tongues, standing before the throne and before the Lamb, clothed in white robes, with palm branches in their hands, and crying out with a loud voice, 'Salvation belongs to our God who sits upon the throne, and to the Lamb!' And all the angels stood round the throne and round the elders and the four living creatures, and they fell on their faces before the throne and worshiped God, saying, 'Amen! Blessing and glory and wisdom and thanksgiving and honor and power and might be to our God for ever and ever! Amen.'

Then one of the elders addressed me, saying, 'Who are these, clothed in white robes, and whence have they come?' I said to him, 'Sir you know.' And he said to me, 'These are they who have come out of the great tribulation; they have washed their robes and made them white in the blood of the Lamb.

Therefore are they before the throne of God,
and serve him day and night within his temple,
and he who sits upon the throne will shelter them with his presence.
They shall hunger no more, neither thirst any more,
the sun shall not strike them, nor any scorching heat.
For the Lamb in the midst of the throne will be their shepherd,
and he will guide them to springs of living water;
and God will wipe away every tear from their eyes.' "

Revelation 7:9-17, RSV

There is an ancient Scottish word "Kythe," which means to communicate with someone, in love, beyond the barriers of time and space.

We pause today for just such a communication. We recognize the great cloud of witnesses by whom we are surrounded—those who have died before us, but from whom we can never be separated.

Minister: With the clear accent of Christian triumph and victory, we remember, these saints.

After the service, the banners are hung in the fellowship hall or narthex, or some other appropriate place in your church. They are displayed for an entire year until the next All Saints Day. At that time they are presented to the families of the deceased and new banners are hung in their place.

Transfiguration
Cloud Meditation and Hike

Religious education involves far more than an hour each week. One of the ways we teach that something is special is by going to a special place. A celebration can be shaped by the environment.

In observing the special day of Transfiguration in our calendar of Christ's life, the entire congregation or selected church school classes go on a field trip to a nearby park with a mountain. The event will include a hike up the mountain and the service of Transfiguration at the mountaintop.

In the liturgical calendar, the celebration of Transfiguration occurs the last Sunday after Epiphany in Episcopal and Lutheran churches and the second Sunday of Lent in Roman Catholic churches. Your learning community should chose a day when hiking will be comfortable. Ideal conditions would be a bright day with clouds.

In preparing for this service, there are certain details to attend to ahead of time.

1. **Plan the location.** If a mountain hike is impossible in your location, can you improvise? Can you use the church property? A nearby recreation area? Be creative! Remember, it is fun to travel as a group from one place to another. take caution that everyone can participate, even those not physically capable. We are seeking a special place—holy ground. Mountains are ideal, but the city or grassland offer possibilities. We are seeking to use the setting to create a moment of fullness where human beings can encounter God.

2. **Check the site** personally to see that it meets all your needs.

3. **Choose** the time.

4. **A letter to those attending** is a good idea, particularly parents of children, telling them where you will be, the time involved, and how to dress.

5. **Arrange transportation.** A church van? Individual cars?

6. **Make arrangements for food.**

7. **Assign responsibilities** for the mountaintop service.

Much will depend on where you hold the celebration. If you are going to be transported to the site, early Sunday afternoon might be a good time to hold your service, concluding with a picnic.

On arrival at the location, explain any rules: e.g., stay with your group as you hike; meet at the top at a designated time; etc.

Now enjoy the hike.

Service of Transfiguration

Begin with singing. There is no need for song books. A leader can line out a new song or use one or more familiar to the group.

Leader: The mountain has often been the meeting place between God and God's people. Moses had a mountaintop experience on Mt. Sinai that shaped his whole understanding of life and mission. Listen to the story:

Reader 1: The Lord said to Moses, "Come up the mountain to me and while you are here I will give you two stone tablets which contain all the laws that I have written for the instruction of the people." Moses and his helper Joshua got ready and Moses began to go up the holy mountain. Moses went up Mt. Sinai and a cloud covered it. The dazzling light of the Lord's presence came down on the mountain. To the Israelites the light looked like a fire burn ing on the top of the mountain. The cloud covered the mountain for six days and on the seventh day the Lord called to Moses from the cloud. Moses went on up the mountain into the cloud.

(Exodus 24:12, 13)

Reader 2: When Moses went down from Mt. Sinai carrying the ten commandments, his face was shining because he had been speaking with the Lord, but he did not know it. Aaron and all the people looked at Moses and saw that his face was shining and they were afraid to go near him.

(Exodus 34:29, 30)

Leader: Throughout history the mountains have been places of meeting God. Often in our daily life we have stripped things of their mystery and numinosity—nothing is holy any longer. But when we go up on the mountain, we see things in a proper perspective and often God speaks to us here. Martin Luther King, Jr., said in his famous speech on the steps of the Washington Monument: "I have been to the mountaintop." Visions are given on mountains. The story that we are celebrating today took place on a mountain. To help us get the feeling level of this story we are going to "cloud fish" as we listen. Lie on your backs or get in any comfortable position that will allow you to see the sky and watch the shape and movement of the clouds. Hear now our story from Mark 9:2-8:

Leader: Six days later Jesus took with him Peter, James, and John and led them up a high mountain, where they were alone. As they looked on, a change came over Jesus and his clothes became shining white—whiter than anyone in the world could wash them.

To Students: Find a cloud that is whiter than anyone could wash. Watch it in silence. Try to move out of the area of thinking and talking and move into the area of feeling and sensing. Keep your eyes half closed, resting on the cloud.

Pause: After a few moments continue reading.

Leader: Then the three disciples saw Elijah and Moses talking with Jesus.

To Students: Look for figures in the clouds. Can you see shapes of persons?

Pause: After a few moments continue reading.

Leader: As they looked on, a change came over Jesus; his face was shining like the sun and his clothes were dazzling white (Matthew 17:2).

To Students: Look for a cloud with the sun behind it, that is shining white. Try to feel relaxed and at peace.

(Pause.)

Leader: Peter spoke up and said to Jesus: "Lord, how good it is that we are here. If you wish I will make three tents here—one for you—one for Moses, one for Elijah." While he was talking a shining cloud came over them and a voice from the cloud said: "This is my own dear son with whom I am pleased. Listen to him."

To Students: Concentrate on the sun and its brightness. Look for an aureole around the cloud.

(Pause.)

Leader: When the disciples heard the voice they were so terrified that they threw themselves face downward on the ground.

To Students: Now shut your eyes tight and cover your face with your hands. Attempt to experience total darkness but be aware of the colors and lights that are still before your eyes.

(Pause: Allow a few moments for this experience.)

Leader: Jesus came to them and touched them. "Get up," he said, "Don't be afraid."

To Students: When you are ready, gently open your eyes.

Leader: So they looked up and saw no one there but Jesus.

To Students: This is one of a series of manifestations by which God authenticated Jesus as his Son (like angels at his birth and a dove at his baptism). Briefly, the veil is drawn aside, and we realize that there are ways of seeing that are beyond mere looking. We use the expression "seeing the light" when we gain insight. Think for a moment on how our lives are transfigured in the light of Christ's presence with us.

(Pause.)

Peter wanted to stay on the mountain. We have had feelings like this. "Lord I don't want this to end. I want always to feel like this. Let me stay here."

To Students: Take just a moment and remember those times in your life. Turn to the person beside you and share a time you wished would never end.

Leader: Those moments *do* end. We can't possess them forever, those special occasions. We can only enjoy them for what they are and for as long as they last and try to learn from them. There are times when we get bogged down in disappointments and confusion. Then we let our minds return to the transfiguration moments. We go cloud-fishing. But we are always called to move on and face the world as it is. We go back down the mountain and into a new experience. A picnic supper is waiting for us.

A Postscript

Liturgical? or non-liturgical churches?

General Bible study? or lectionary reading?

Formal or informal church school?

However different our styles, we share, by God's mercy, an enormous common ground. We all focus on Jesus, his birth, death, and resurrection. We have human feelings in common and a universal yearning of God.

Understanding and living out the Church Year is but one method of expressing the commonality. It is a vehicle to carry us to our ultimate goal, union with God.

The Church Year is a path Christians of different traditions can journey together hand-in-hand, gaining fellowship with one another without losing any special denominational value and without departing from our New Testament faith.

> Jesus, united by thy grace,
> And each to each endeared,
> With confidence we seek thy face,
> And know our prayer is heard.
>
> Touched by the lodestone of thy love,
> Let all our hearts agree;
> And ever toward each other move,
> And ever move toward thee.
>
> Charles Wesley

Other popular Christian Education resources by Judy Gattis Smith!

Teaching to Wonder *Spiritual Growth Through Imagination and Movement*
ISBN 0-687-41123-8

Developing a Child's Spiritual Growth through Sight, Sound, Taste, Touch & Smell
ISBM 0-687-10499-8

26 Ways to Use Drama in Teaching the Drama
ISBN 0-687-42745-2

Teaching with Music Through the Church Year
ISBM 0-687-41133-5

The books listed above by Judy Gattis Smith are part of the Griggs Educational Resources Series from Abingdon Press. This popular series is already helping more than 300,000 Christian educators develop effective programs for their churches. A complete list of Griggs Educational Resources follows.

The Griggs Educational Resources Series

Basic Skills for Church Teachers
ISBN 0-687-02488-9

The Church-Related Preschool
ISBN 0-687-08334-6

Creative Activities in Church Education
ISBN 0-687-09812-2

Developing a Child's Spiritual Growth Through Sight, Sound, Taste, Touch, Smell
ISBM 0-687-10499-8

Developing Christian Education in the Smaller Church
ISBN 0-687-10508-0

Journey to Jerusalem
ISBN 0-687-20593-X

Opening the Bible with Children
ISBN 0-687-29210-7

Praying and Teaching the Psalms
ISBN 0-687-33633-3

Preparing for the Messiah
ISBN 0-687-33920-0

Teaching and Celebrating Advent
ISBN 0-687-41080-0

Teaching and Celebrating Lent-Easter
ISBN 0-687-41081-9

Teaching Prayer in the Classroom
ISBN 0-687-41100-9

Teaching Teachers to Teach
ISBN 0-687-41120-3

Teaching to Wonder
ISBN 0-687-41123-8

Teaching with Music Through the Church Year
ISBN 0-687-41133-5

20 New Ways of Teaching the Bible
ISBN 0-687-42740-1

26 Ways to Use Drama in Teaching the Bible
ISBN 0-687-42745-2

Using Computers in Religious Education
ISBN 0-687-43120-4

Using Storytelling in Christian Education
ISBN 0-687-43117-4

Where Faith Seeks Understanding
ISBN 0-687-45173-6

Youth Ministries: Thinking Big with Small Groups
ISBN 0-687-47203-2

Call toll free 1-800-672-1789 for price information.

Order from your bookstore, which may call toll free 1-800-251-3320. Individual customers call toll free 1-800-672-1789 or write Cokesbury Service Center / 825 Sixth Ave. South / Nashville, TN 37203

Notes